AMERICAN ORIENTAL SERIES
ESSAY 5

HISTORY OF EGYPT

An Extract from
IBN TAGHRĪ BIRDĪ'S
Ḥawādith ad-Duhūr
A.D. 1441–1450

AMERICAN ORIENTAL SERIES

AMERICAN ORIENTAL SOCIETY

NEW HAVEN, CONNECTICUT

1967

HISTORY OF EGYPT

An Extract From

ABŪ L-MAḤĀSIN IBN TAGHRĪ BIRDĪ'S CHRONICLE

Entitled

Ḥawādith ad-Duhūr fī Maḍā l-'Ayyām wash-Shuhūr

(845-854 A.H., A.D. 1441-1450)

Translated from the Arabic by

WILLIAM POPPER (d. 1963)

Prepared for publication and edited by

WALTER J. FISCHEL

AN
ESSAY
OF THE
AMERICAN ORIENTAL SOCIETY

No. 5

This work has been printed with the aid of a subvention from the Graduate Division of the University of California, Berkeley.

PRINTED IN THE UNITED STATES OF AMERICA
BY WAVERLY PRESS, INC., BALTIMORE, MARYLAND

EDITOR'S NOTE

After having accomplished the translation into English of Ibn Taghrī Birdī's *an-Nujūm az-Ẓahira* for the years 1382–1469, William Popper turned to the other historical work of Ibn Taghrī Birdī, known as *Ḥawādith ad-Duhūr* with the intention to render also this chronicle of Egypt into English on the basis of his own edition of the Arabic text.

The Arabic text of the *Ḥawādith* as edited by William Popper and published in Volume 8 of the *University of California Publications in Semitic Philology* (Berkeley-Los Angeles, 1930–1942) covered the years from A.D. 1441 to 1470 (845–874 H.) of the history of Mamlūk Egypt.

Professor Popper had started the English translation of the *Ḥawādith*, and had carried it on from the year A.D. 1441 until the middle of A.D. 1450 of the rule of the Mamlūk Sultan Jaqmaq. His death on June 3, 1963, however, prevented him from completing this last phase of his manifold scholarly activities.

Among his papers was found the unfinished manuscript of this English portion of the *Ḥawādith*, corresponding to the Arabic edition of Volume 8, pp. 1–85.

The editor took it upon himself to prepare this manuscript for publication, to compare it with the Arabic original, to check every item, name, title, and term, while fully adhering to William Popper's method of translating and transliterating Arabic texts as so masterly manifested by him in his previous publications.[1]

The editor submits herewith Professor Popper's last piece of scholarly work, as an expression of his devotion to his revered colleague and noble friend and as a tribute to so great a scholar and gentleman.

UNIVERSITY OF CALIFORNIA
BERKELEY

WALTER J. FISCHEL

[1] For an evaluation of William Popper's works see my study "William Popper (1874–1963) and his Contribution to Islamic Scholarship" in *Journal of the American Oriental Society*, 84, 1964, pp. 213–20.

SULTAN AL-MALIK AẒ-ẒĀHIR JAQMAQ: 845–854 A.H.

A.D. 1441 *Year 845 A.H.*

VIII, 1 May 22, When this year began the Caliph was al-Mu'taḍid Billāh Abu l'Fatḥ Dā'ud; he was sick. The Sultan of Egypt, of the territory of Ḥijāz and Syria, was Abū Sa'īd Jaqmaq. The Cadis were: Shāfi'ite, the memorizer of the age Shihāb (ad-Dīn Aḥmad) ibn Ḥajar al-'Asqalānī; Ḥanafite, Sa'd ad-Dīn ibn Dairī; Mālikite, Badr ad-Dīn (Aḥmad) ibn at-Tanasī; Ḥanbalite, Badr ad-Dīn (Muḥammad ibn 'Abd al-Mun'im) al-Baghdādī. The market inspector of Cairo was Badr ad-Dīn Maḥmūd al-'Ainī.

The emirs were: commander-in-chief Yashbak as-Sūdūnī al-Mushidd; emir of arms, Timrāz al-Qirmishī aẓ-Ẓāhirī Barqūq; emir of the council, Jarbāsh Qāshuq; grand emir of the horse, Qarā Khujā al-Ḥasanī; chief head of guards, Tamurbāi at-Tamurbughāwī; grand chamberlain, Tanbak al-Bardbakī; grand executive secretary, Taghrī Birdī al-Baklamishī al-Mu'dhī; head of emirs of the first class, Nāṣir ad-Dīn Muḥammad, son of Sultan (Jaqmaq); also a number of others including all the office holders mentioned above and others, the number of emirs of the first class being
VIII, 2 twelve, a half of the number in past ages. As for the office of (grand) treasurer, this had been abolished by al-Ashraf Barsbāi in the year 831 when he vacated the fief of Qarā Murād Khujā ash-Shā'bānī aẓ-Ẓāhirī Barqūq and banished him to Jerusalem; the position (of treasurer) is now administered by one of the enlisted free troopers whose name need not be mentioned here; the treasurer (i.e., the former second treasurer), Qānibak al-Ashrafī, an emir of the third class, who was sick; superintendent of the buttery, Qānibāi al-Jarkasī, an emir of the second class; warden of the armory, Taghrī Birmish as-Saifī Yashbak ibn Uzdamur; viceroy of the Citadel, Mamjiq an-Naurūzī; second emir of the horse, Jarbāsh Kurd; second head of guards, Yalkhujā min Māmish an-Nāṣirī as-Sāqī; second chamberlain, Sūdūn as-Sūdūnī aẓ-Ẓāhirī Barqūq; second executive secretary, Daulāt Bāi al-Mu'ayyadī; chief eunuch of the palace, aṣ-Ṣafi Jauhar al-Qunuqbāi; commander of the Sultan's mamlūks, 'Abd al-Laṭīf al-Manjakī ar-Rūmī, known as al-'Uthmānī; deputy commander of the mamlūks Jauhar al-Manjakī; governor (of Cairo) Qarājā al-'Umarī.

Bureau Officials: Confidential secretary, Kamāl ad-Dīn ibn al-Barīzī; controller of the army, Muḥibb ad-Dīn ibn al-Ashqar;

vizier, Karīm ad-Dīn ibn Kātib al-Manākh; major-domo, Qīz
Ṭūghān al-ʿAlāʾī; controller of privy funds Jamāl ad-Dīn Yūsuf
VIII, 3 ibn Kātib Jakam; deputy confidential secretary, Sharaf ad-Dīn
al-Ashqar; controller of financial bureaus, Amīn ad-Dīn Ibrāhīm
ibn al-Haiṣam; controller of the special bureau, Zain ad-Dīn
Yaḥyā al-Ashqar; controller of the stables, Taqī ad-Dīn ibn Naṣr
Allāh; scribe of the bureau of mamlūks, Faraj ibn Mājid ibn an-
Naḥḥāl.

Damascus: Julbān as-Saifī Ināl Ḥaṭab, known as Amīr Ākhūr; Aleppo: Qānibāi al-Hamzāwī; Ṭarābulus: Barsbāi al-Bāṣirī al-Ḥajīb; Ḥamā: Bardbak al-Jakamī al-ʿAjamī al-Aʿwar; Ṣafad: Qānibāi al-Abū Bakrī an-Nāṣirī, known as al-Bahlawān; Gaza: Ṭūkh al-Abūbakrī al-Mu'ayyadī; al-Karak: Māzī aẓ-Ẓāhirī Barqūq; Malaṭya: Khalīl ibn Shāhīn ash-Shaikhī; Jerusalem: Ṭūghān al-ʿUthmānī; Ḥimṣ: Baighūt min Ṣafer Khujā al-Mu' ayyadī al-Aʿraj.

May — Muḥarram 1, 845 A.H. was a Sunday (Monday). Nothing (im-
June 20 — portant) occurred in this month. Similarly in the month of Ṣafar.

I Rabīʿi was a Wednesday (Thursday). On the first the Nile completed 16 cubits, and Nāṣir ad-Dīn Muḥammad, the Sultan's son, went down from the Citadel until he crossed the Nile, perfumed the nilometer, returned and opened the (Cairo) Canal dam, mounted again and ascended to the Citadel. His father, as was the custom, invested him with a magnificent robe. Ṣalāḥ ad-Dīn aṣ-Ṣafadī was the author of the verses (on this rise of the Nile).

Thursday, end of the month. ʿIzz ad-Dīn ʿAbd al-ʿAzīz al-Baghdādī was appointed Ḥanbalite Cadi of Damascus in place of Zain ad-Din ʿUmar ibn Mufliḥ because of the latter's removal.

*VIII, 4 — II Rabīʿ: Nothing happened in this month.

Aug. 19–Sept. 16 — * I Jumādā began on a Sunday.

Sept. 17–Oct. 17 — II Jumādā began on a Tuesday.

Nov. 15 — Rajab began on a Wednesday.

A.D. 1442

Year 846 A.H.

The year began with all officials in their previously noted positions except the Caliph, who was al-Mustakfī Billāh Abū ar-Rabīʿ Sulaimān.

May 12 — Muḥarram began on a Friday (Saturday).

May 19 — Saturday, Muḥarram 9 (8). Shaikh ʿAlī al-Mālikī, who had earlier come from Damascus, was appointed to the Cadiship of Alexandria.

June 17 — Ṣafar 1 was a Sunday (Monday).

June 18 Monday, Ṣafar 9. An individual named Ḥamīd ad-Dīn, one of the descendants of the Imām (Abū Ḥanīfa) was appointed Ḥanafite Cadi in Damascus after the removal of Shams ad-Dīn aṣ-Ṣafadī.

June 25 (Ṣafar 16). The report (concerning the uprising of the purchased mamlūks) reached the Sultan, who sent to them the commander of the mamlūks, the eunuch 'Abd al-Laṭīf, to discuss with them the settlement of their affairs. But they refused, insisted on rioting and made demands impossible to grant; they persisted in their course of action, in that [they permitted] the men only rarely to enter to the Sultan. Their attitude grew worse until the veteran mamlūks who were in Cairo were openly against them, though their secret feelings belong to God alone. They continued in this
June 27 attitude until the eve of Wednesday [Ṣafar 18] when they broke open the door of the armory and took from it a huge number of weapons. This was reported to the Sultan who summoned the veteran mamlūks to come to him at the Gate of the Chain and sent them to fight them [the purchased mamlūks]. The emirs who were present tried to restrain the Sultan and warned him of the
VIII, 5 result of his proposed action, nor did the veterans agree with him in regard to the task to which he was sending them because they knew that at the end it would not be an easy task for them.

In the meanwhile the purchased mamlūks were continuing to prevent the men from ascending [to the Sultan] until the Sultan summoned the confidential secretary Ibn al-Bārizī, but he was unable to ascend from the Steps Gate, so he tried to go up from the gate of the Race Course which is below the Citadel; but some of the purchased and veteran mamlūks perceived him and struck him with a mace intending to kill him, but one of the bystanders came to his aid and set him free, so that he was able to spur his horse; with blood on his garments from a head wound which he had received, he went up to the Citadel in a state of agitation. In the meantime the most extreme vilifications and insults had been directed against their master by the mamlūks. This continued
June 29 until Friday the 20th [19th]; then the uprising ended because of dissension among them.

July 10 I Rabī' began on a Tuesday.

July 23 Monday, I Rabī' 14. The Nile reached plenitude, and His Highness Nāṣir ad-Dīn Muḥammad, the Sultan's son, went down from the Citadel with the leaders of the government, crossed the Nile, perfumed the Nilometer, then opened the Canal of the Dam and rode to the Citadel, where his father invested him with an overcloak with a border of gold embroidery. Ibn an-Naqīb has some excellent verses containing a quotation from another poem, in basīṭ measure.

July 30 Monday, I Rabī' 21. The Sultan sent Taghrī-Birmish* as-Saifī
*VIII, 6 Yashbak ibn Uzdamur, warden of the armory, to make his prep-

arations and proceed to besiege Caesarea, taking with him the weapons of war and siege, including cannon, ballisters, etc., and he gave him 500 dīnārs. After some days he journeyed to Aleppo, then returned to Egypt without going to Caesarea or elsewhere.

Aug. 9 II Rabī' 1 was a Wednesday (Thursday).

Aug. 30 On the eve of Thursday, the 23rd (22nd), a number of the mamlūks of Taghrī Birdī al-Mu'dhī, the grand executive secretary, were arrested; they had determined to kill their master and detained him this night until the day rose. This was reported to the Sultan, who sent to them a number of heads of guards; they seized a large number of them and gave them a painful beating, then their master sent them under the governor (of Cairo) to the Maqshara Prison.

(II Rabī' 27) Ibn ar-Rassām was appointed controller of the army of Aleppo after the removal of Zain ad-Dīn 'Umar as-Saffāḥ.

Sept. 14 Friday, I Jumādā 9 (8). Zain ad-Dīn ibn al-Kuwaiz journeyed to Jerusalem out of service, after there had been taken from him a large amount of gold.

Sept. 16 Sunday, the 11th (10th). Cadi Nūr ad-Dīn 'Alī ibn Salīm, a deputy Shāfi'te Cadi, was appointed to the office of Cadi of Ṣafad.

Sept. 23 Sunday, the 18th (17th). The Sultan summoned the treasurer, the executive secretary, and the head of guards of Taghrī Birmish, viceroy of Aleppo, and gave them a painful beating, then ordered them banished to Syria. He then ordered the scribe of the mamlūks
VIII, 7 to erase the names of the twelve mamlūks who had previously been designated to go to Mecca, because of their failure to appear on the day of review. Then one of the emirs interceded for them, and he restored them to their former position.

Oct. 7 II Jumādā 1 was a Saturday.

Oct. 8 Sunday, II Jumādā 2. 'Alā' ad-Dīn ibn Aqbars, controller of pious trust foundations, was illegally invested as Shaikh of the Qūṣūn Monastery in the Smaller Qarāfā, in place of Mu'īn ad-Dīn 'Abd al-Laṭīf ibn al-Ashqar, deputy private secretary.

Oct. 14 Saturday, the 8th. The gift of Julbān, the viceroy of Damascus, arrived and was brought to the Sultan; it included about 200 horses, of which three were with saddles of gold and (brocade) housings; ten mamlūks; many pieces of wool and fur; garments of Ba'albakkī linen and satin; some bows; and 10,000 dinars, according to reports.

Nov. 5 Rajab 1 was a Monday.

Nov. 26 Monday, the 22nd. The Shaikh of Islām (Shihāb ad-Dīn Aḥmad) ibn Ḥajar was appointed Shaikh of the Tomb of ash-Shāfi'ī after the removal of 'Alā' ad-Dīn al-Qalqashandī.

Nov. 29 Thursday, the 25th. A number of Arabs of the Najd came to

Cairo; the Sultan had summoned them to appoint their chief Emir of Medina, as a rebuff to the infidels, since they (the Arabs of the Najd) were Sunnites. The Sultan lodged them on the Race Course and showed them honor, but what he wished he did not attain because of the wishes of some of the officials.

Dec. 5 Sha'bān 1 was a Tuesday (Wednesday). On this day the ambassadors of the sons of Shāh Rukh, the son of Tamerlane, came to Cairo and the Sultan arranged for them a service in the Great Castle of the Citadel, cancelling the service in the Great Pontico.

*VIII, 8 * Shawwāl 1 was a Saturday.

Feb. 2

Feb. 16 Monday, (Dhu l-Qa'da), 15. Shaikh of Islām, Ibn Ḥajar, was
A.D. 1443 ordered to remain in his home. And Taqī ad-Dīn 'Abd ar-Raḥmān ibn Tāj ad-Dīn ibn Naṣr Allāh was appointed controller of the stables in place of Shams ad-Dīn Naṣr Allāh, known as al-Wazza.

April 11 On Thursday the Shaikh of Islām, Ibn Ḥajar, was restored to his position as Cadi.

Dhu l-Ḥijja 1 was a Tuesday.

April 15 Monday, the 14th. Ṭūghān al-'Uthmānī, former viceroy of Jerusalem, was restored to that position after he had been mulcted and banished to Aleppo.

Year 847 A.H.

The year 847 began with everything as it had been in the previous year except that the grand executive secretary was Īnāl al-'Alā'ī an-Nāṣirī.

Muḥarram 1 was a Thursday (Wednesday).

May 3 Friday, Muḥarram 2 (3). The Sultan ordered the imprisonment in the Maqshara of the Europeans arriving from Rhodes, and a number of Christians; and all were imprisoned there.

May 11 Saturday, Muḥarram 10 [11]. Sirāj ad-Dīn al-Ḥimṣī was appointed Shāfi'ite Cadi in Tripoli after the removal of Shihāb ad-Dīn ibn az-Zahrī; and Sirāj ad-Dīn was given also the appointment as controller of the army of Tripoli.

May 1–10 First days of Muḥarram. Jamāl ad-Dīn al-Bā'ūnī was trans-
VIII, 9 ferred to the office of Cadi of Damascus after the removal of Shams ad-Dīn al-Wanā'ī, and Shams ad-Dīn Ibn al-Kharazī was appointed Cadi of Aleppo.

July 29 II Rabī' 1 was a Monday.

Aug. 3 Saturday, the 6th. The Nile reached plenitude and His Highness Nāṣir ad-Dīn went down, perfumed the Nilometer and opened the Dam as usual; then he was invested. [On this occasion] an-Naṣīr al-Munāwī was the author of verses [3 lines in kāmil meter].

Aug. 29 I Jumādā 1 was a Tuesday.

On this day there arrived 'Umar ibn as-Saffāḥ, Ḥaṭaṭ an-Nāṣirī, viceroy of the citadel of Aleppo, and Gharīb, the Sultan's
VIII, 10 major domo there, in response to a summons from him. When they stood before him he put them under the charge of Taghrī Birmish al-Faqīh, viceroy of the Citadel, and ordered him to treat them harshly, keep them under guard and imprison them in the Tower. He [Taghrī Birmish] took them home with him and demanded of them the money belonging to Taghrī Birmish, viceroy of Aleppo, which they had used when he rebelled and went against the Sultan. The amount demanded by the Sultan from Ibn as-Saffāḥ was 30,000 dīnārs, from Ḥaṭaṭ, 50,000 dīnārs, and from the other, about the same amount. They remained in confinement for a time until there had been taken from them a large sum.

Aug. 31 Then on Saturday, the 5th [of I Jumādā], Ibn ar-Rassām was appointed confidential secretary, controller of the army, and controller of the citadel, in Aleppo, in place of Ibn as-Saffāḥ, because of his removal and mulcting, and Shāhīn aṭ-Ṭūghānī al-Ashqar, former executive secretary of the Sultan, and now third executive secretary was appointed viceroy of the citadel of Aleppo in place of Ḥaṭaṭ, because of his removal and mulcting also.

Sept. 12 Thursday, the 17th. Amīn ad-Dīn 'Abd ar-Raḥmān ibn ad-Dairī was appointed controller of the two holy places, Jerusalem and Hebron, on payment of a sum of money which he promised to pay after the death of Ghars ad-Dīn Khalīl as-Sākhāwī.

Sept. 23 Monday, the 28th. Cadi 'Izz ad-Dīn ibn al-Bisāṭī al-Mālikī was appointed Cadi of Damascus in place of Yaḥyā al-Maghribī because of his removal.

Sept. 26 II Jumādā 1 was a Wednesday (Thursday).

Sept. 28 Saturday, the 4th (3rd). 'Izz ad-Dīn, mentioned above, was removed as Cadi of Damascus.

Oct. 22 Monday, the 27th (26th). The ambassador of Qa'ān Mu'īn ad-Dīn Shāh Rukh ibn Tīmūr Lank and the ambassador of Jahān
VIII, 11 Shāh ibn Qarā Yūsuf, arrived in Cairo.

Rajab 1 was a Friday.

A.D. 1444 Sha'bān and Ramaḍān: nothing happened in these two months.

Jan. 22 Shawwāl 1 was a Wednesday.

Feb. 19 Wednesday, Shawwāl 29. Badr ad-Dīn Muḥammad ibn Fatḥ ad-Dīn Ṣadaqa al-Maḥarraqī was appointed controller of tributes in place of his father because of the latter's weakness and old age; similarly he was appointed to the rest of his father's positions.

Year 848 A.H.

The year began with [all] officials in their previous positions, and prices medium: the price of the gold dīnār was 285 dirhams in exchange and 90 in business transactions; the ducat was five dirhams cheaper than the Ashrafī [dīnār] among importers: the gold mithqāl was at 335, the silver dirham at 24 coppers [fulūs], and the dirham of coppers was at eight pieces [of copper] mixed with brass and other [metal]. Wheat in the middle of the past century had been at 300 dirhams per irdabb and was now at 200 or less. The prices of other commodities were cheap, though the plague had begun to appear at the beginning of Dhu l-Ḥijja of the past year and was now at the beginning of this year, spreading—we ask God for a happy ending!

April 20 Muḥarram 1 was a Monday. On this day the plague spread, and began to increase one day and diminish the next, until the increase became gradually greater, and the number of deaths reached more than 300 a day.

May 1 Friday, the 12th. Shaikh 'Alī al-Khurāsānī, the market inspector, raided the presses on the Būlāq shore; the slaves swarmed
VIII, 12 against him, stoned and almost killed him; had he not sought refuge in the home of Kamāl ad-Dīn Ibn al-Bārizī, the confidential secretary, he would have perished.

May 20 Ṣafar 1 was a Wednesday.

May 21 Thursday, the 2nd. Ibn Ẓahīr was appointed controller of pious trust foundations in place of 'Alā' ad-Dīn 'Alī ibn Aqbars because of the latter's removal from office.

June 18 I Rabī' 1 was a Friday [Thursday]. On this day the Sultan banished Yūnus, emir of the horse.

June 21 Sunday, I Rabī' 3 [4]. The Sultan beat al-Muḥibb Abu l-Barakāt al-Haitamī, one of the deputy (cadis) and imprisoned him in the Maqshara for no reason justifying this. When the Shaikh of Islam, Ibn Ḥajar, heard of this he removed himself (from his office), but afterward the Sultan restored him to the office and released the Abu l-Barakāt mentioned above.

June 27 Saturday, I Rabī' 9 (10). The Sultan banished to Aleppo Sūdūn, a mamlūk of Ṭughān, former emir of the horse. Had he sent this Sūdūn further away, it would have been better.

During these days the Sultan ordered the banishment of Shaikh Shams ad-Dīn Muḥammad ibn al-'Aṭṭār al-Ḥanafī, one of the Ṣūfīs of the Shaikhūn Monastery, to Malaṭyā. Shams ad-Dīn went out from Cairo until he reached Siryāqaus Monastery; then intercession was made for him, and he returned to Cairo in his former position. The cause in all this was Shams ad-Dīn (Muḥammad al-Ḥanafī ar-Rūmī, known as) the Scribe, for he had a bad influence on the Sultan. As far as Shams ad-Dīn ibn al-'Aṭṭār is concerned, he was one of the best of men and one of the foremost Ḥanafite jurists.

July 20 (Monday, II Rabī' 31). On this date also the Sultan ordered Emir Shādibak al-Jakamī and Tūkh min Timrāz, called Bīnī

Bāziq (meaning "thick of neck"), both of whom were emirs of the first class in Egypt, to travel to Upper Egypt in order to repel
VIII, 13 the Bedouin marauders; previously he had sent to Upper Egypt Aitamish min Azūbāi al-Mu'ayyadī, the chief steward, with fifty of the Sultan's mamlūks, but Aitamish and those with him had been unable to resist the Bedouins, who were Kunūz Arabs.

Aug. 1 Saturday, II Rabī' 15. Sūdūn al-Bardbakī, emir of the armor bearers and one of the chamberlains, was appointed viceroy of Damietta fortress; he was invested on Monday in place of Saif ad-Dīn Ṭūghān as-Saifī Āqbirdī al-Minqār because of Ṭūghān's removal from office and departure to Syria as an emir.

Tuesday, the 18th. Daulāt Bāi, the second executive secretary, was appointed controller of the Azhar Mosque.

The Nile reached plenitude; and his Highness Fakhr ad-Dīn 'Uthmān, son of Sultan Jaqmaq, went down from the Citadel with the leaders of the government, the emirs and others, until he crossed the Nile, perfumed the Nilometer, returned and opened the Cairo Canal, mounted and ascended to the Citadel; his father invested him as usual with an outer robe with gold embroidery. One of the poets composed verses (on the occasion of this plenitude).

Aug. 16 The two Jumādās: Nothing occurred in these two months.
Sept. 14

Oct. 14 Rajab 1 was a Wednesday.

Oct. 15 Thursday, Rajab 2. A number of heads of the Bedouin Kunūz Arabs, carried on spears, arrived in Cairo.

Oct. 17 (Rajab 4). Bardbak al-'Ajamī was imprisoned because of what he had done, for some reason or other, to the people of Ḥamā, when he used harsh language toward them, so that they were dis-
VIII, 14 affected toward him, and hostility resulted between them, fighting took place, and Bardbak, with his mamlūks, rode against them and fought them until a number of them (more than 120) had been killed, mostly in cold blood, while of his party only four or less were killed. When this happened to him, he revolted, left his allegiance and went down to the desert of Ḥamā, where he remained for some days. But he was not successful, and Julbān, viceroy of Damascus, acted as a mediator and asked for a safe-conduct from him. He questioned the Sultan on this subject, and the Sultan sent him (Bardbak) the safe-conduct and he came (to Cairo).

Nov. 13 Sha'bān 1 was a Thursday (Friday). On Monday, the 12th (11th) 'Alī Bāi al-Ashrafī arrived at Cairo; from the time that he was captured and imprisoned, then freed, he had been out of service in Syria and had not been in Cairo.

Nov. 30 Monday, the 19th (18th). Bahā' ad-Dīn ibn Ḥijjī, controller of the army of Damascus, came to Cairo, went up to the Sultan, who invested him with a Kāmilīya robe with a sable fur.

Dec. 1 Tuesday, the 21st (19th). The gift of Qānibāi al-Ḥamzāwī, viceroy of Aleppo, arrived with its executive secretary Saif ad-Dīn Taghrī Birmish; it consisted of 100 horses and a number of crates containing various kinds of furs, colored wool, satin, Ba'albakkī (cotton), etc.

Dec. 12 Ramaḍān 1 was a Friday (Saturday). On this day Bahā' ad-Dīn ibn Ḥijjī went up to the Sultan to be appointed to the office of controller of the army in Egypt, but this (appointment) was not effected.

*VIII, 15 *Shawwāl 1 was a Sunday (Monday).

Jan. 11

Jan. 19 Tuesday, Shawwāl 10 (9). Sirāj ad-Dīn al-Ḥimṣī was appointed A.D. 1445 Shāfi'ite Cadi in Aleppo in place of Ibn al-Kharazī because of the latter's removal.

Jan. 25 [Monday, Shawwāl 16 (15). A report arrived from Murād Bak] that there had taken place between him and a party of the Banu l-Aṣfar (Greeks) a great battle the like of which had not been witnessed in these days, in that there had been killed in the battle more than 10,000 persons, while of the Banū Aṣfar the number killed was unlimited; finally God had aided the Mohammedans against the Greeks and they had made captives among them, killed, taken prisoners and seized booty (in vast amounts), thank God! And Ibn 'Uthmān took captive five of the important Banu l-Aṣfar mentioned above who had authority in their realms; and the Mohammedans, beside the more than 10,000 prisoners which they took from the Greeks, had seized exceedingly vast amounts of property.

Thursday, the 19th [18th]. The emir of the pilgrimage, Tamurbāi at-Tamurbughāwī, went out to Pilgrim's Lake; the emir of the advance pilgrimage was Qānim at-Tājir [al-Mu'ayyadī, an emir of the third class.]

[In 848 A.H., in Rajab, the Sultan had abolished the customary exercise of the lancers during the pilgrimage parade;] the people were intensely incensed, despite the promise he had previously made to restore the practice.

Jan. 26 Tuesday, the 16th [of Shawwāl]. Zain ad-Dīn Yaḥyā, the majordomo, sent to the Sultan a huge gift containing 300 Arab horses.

Feb. 2 Tuesday, the 21st [23rd]. The ambassador of Murād Bak ibn 'Uthmān, ruler of the land of Byzantium arrived bringing with him a number of the captives which he had taken; their entry to
VIII, 16 Cairo was a memorable day. The ambassador also narrated what we have stated above concerning the battle and reported that Ibn

'Uthmān had sent the like of those captives to a number of the kings of other regions.

Year 849 A.H.

When the year began the officials were the same as in the preceeding year.

Apr. 9 Muḥarram 1 was a Friday.

Apr. 16 Friday eve, Muḥarram 8. The minaret of the old Fakhrīya Mosque near the Slave Market inside Cairo fell upon the caravansary next to it and upon a number of buildings; a vast number of human beings were killed in the fall, and when the Sultan heard of this he inquired who was its [the mosque's] controller and was told "Nūr ad-Dīn al-Qalyūbī", one of the Shāfi'ite deputy cadis and a trust officer of the judiciary. The Sultan immediately summoned him [Nūr ad-Dīn] and ordered that he be halved at the waist; but intercession was made for him, one of the interceders being the grand executive secretary Īnāl al-'Alā'ī; [the Sultan accepted the intercession] after he had cursed and imprecated him and fined him a large sum for its reconstruction. The Sultan then turned to the Shāfi'ite Cadi and addressed him in harsh words which it would be shameful to repeat and he removed him on the spot from the office of Cadi, appointing in his place [Muḥammad ibn 'Alī ibn Muḥammad] al-Qāyātī. The Sultan was not blamed for what he had done in regard to the Cadi and his deputy; for the concern of the judiciary includes failure to attend to the construction of the pious foundations and university mosques whose controllership they administer; and I do not know what excuse they will offer therefore before God the Mighty and Exalted or what other apology will be to Him. For this is something which is considered abominable even in an ignorant plebeian, how much the more then in jurists and Cadis: And this has become general
VIII, 17 knowledge in the provinces concerning the Cadis of our time; and most men, when they establish a foundation for a mosque, a hospice, or something similar give the controllership thereof to the chamberlain, or the executive secretary or the chief eunuch and do not give it to a turbanwearer [Cadi] because of the certainty of their conviction that they [the Cadis] would not attend to the welfare of the controllerships—there is no strength or power except in God!

May 1 Saturday, Muḥarram 23. The emir of the litter caravan Tamurbāi [at-Tamurbughāwī] arrived in Cairo.

May 3 Monday, the 25th. The Sultan became angry at Qarājā al-'Umarī an-Nāṣirī, the former governor and emir of this year's

Rajab caravan, and ordered his expulsion to Aleppo because of his evil conduct on the Pilgrimage and elsewise.

May 9 Ṣafar 1 was a Sunday.

May 10 Monday, Ṣafar 2. Māmāi as-Saifi Baibughā al-Muẓaffarī, one of the assistant executive secretaries, was invested [with a robe] and ordered to proceed to Ṭarābulus in order to make a reckoning with the controller of its army, Yūsuf ibn Mūsā al-Karakī, in regard to the Sultan's effects under his control.

June 7 I Rabī' 1 was a Monday.

June 28 Monday, the 22nd. Zain ad-Dīn Yaḥyā the major-domo set out for the region of Bilbais with a large number of the Sultan's mamlūks to fight the Arabs who had revolted.

July 7 II Rabī' 1 was a Wednesday.

July 24 Saturday, the 18th. Zain ad-Dīn, mentioned above, arrived at Cairo, with a large number of Arabs.

In the last decade of the month a woman who lived near the Ibn Ṭūlūn Mosque gave birth to a daughter who had two heads, one above the other, one of them with hair, the other without hair.

*VIII, 18 *Tuesday, I Jumādā 20. Al-Qāyātī ash-Shāfi'ī was appointed
Aug. 24 Shaikh of the Baibarsīya Monastery in place of Shaikh of Islam [Shihāb ad-Dīn] Ibn Ḥajar because of the latter's removal.

Aug. 28 Saturday, the 24th [of II Jumādā]. The Sultan sent Sharīf 'Alī ibn Ḥasan ibn 'Ajlān from the tower [in the Citadel] to the Alexandria prison.

Aug. 29 Sunday, the 25th. Baibars ibn Baqar, shaikh of the Bedouin Arabs in the Eastern Province [of Egypt] was imprisoned in the tower of the Citadel for reasons for which the Sultan bore a grudge against him, anciently and anew.

In the first days of this month the Nile reached plenitude, and His Highness Fakhr ad-Dīn 'Uthmān, son of the Sultan, went down and opened the Cairo Canal according to custom; [then he returned to the Citadel] and his father invested him [with a robe].

Aṣ-Ṣafadī recited on this occasion [two verses in kāmil meter with the rhyming words: *wa-a'shaq* and *tumlaq*].

Sept. 4 II Jumādā 1 was a Saturday.

Thursday, Sha'bān 3. Qānibāi al-Jārkasī had become grand executive secretary and had received the fief of an emir first-class in addition to that of superintendent of the buttery, which he retained in addition to his fief as executive secretary.

Dec. 1 Ramaḍān 1 was a Wednesday.

Dec. 11 Saturday, the 11th. Muḥibb ad-Dīn ibn al-Ashqar, controller of the army, was appointed Shaikh of the Ṣarghatmish College-Mosque after the death of Ibn at-Tafhanī.

Dec. 31 Shawwāl 1 was a Thursday [Friday].

Jan. 1 Saturday, Shawwāl 3[2]. The gift of Muḥammad Bak ibn Murād
1446 A.D. Bak ibn 'Uthmān arrived in Cairo, brought by his ambassador. The ambassador reported that his father [Murād Bak] had relinquished his government to this son of his and established him in his own stead, and had sent to inform the Sultan of this fact; furthermore, that the son would be under the charge of the Sultan.*

*VIII, 19 Monday, the 12th [11th]. The Maghribians sent their gifts to
Jan. 10 the Sultan, thirty horses, most of them mares, and including also other articles.

I made the pilgrimage in this year, as a captain (bāsh) in the litter [caravan]; 'Alī Bāi al-Ashrafī was a captain in the advance pilgrimage.

Jan. 29 Dhu l-Qa'da 1 was a Saturday.

Feb. 12 Saturday, the fifteenth. Zain ad-Dīn, the major-domo, sent to the Sultan 400 horses, of which 60 were with ornamented saddles and 40 with plain saddles.

On this day also a band of mischief-making mamlūks numbering more than 20 individuals went to the homes of the Christians to seize mules from them; but the men sprang upon them, while the Christians defended their homes, and a battle ensued in which three of the mamlūks were killed—to Hell!

Feb. 28 Dhu l-Ḥijja 1 was a Monday.

In this month a strange event occurred, namely, that the slaves, that is, the grooms who were in the spring grazing grounds on the Jīza bank of the Nile, and in Minbāba, when they took their masters' horses there and had remained there a little while, appointed from their own midst a slave whom they made Sultan, appointed for him government officials and holders of official positions, while he made among them decisions as he wished. They erected for him a throne upon which he sat and continued to do as he pleased without anyone able to resist him, until another one of the slaves rebelled against him, both of them gathered recruits, and they fought until the one who had become Sultan was victorious and halved at the waist a number of the other party. The master of the slave who had been killed was unable to say anything,
VIII, 20 though it is said that he went and spoke to the slave who had been made Sultan—some of the men say that he desired to halve him also at the waist, and some say that he placated him with the amount of the slave's money value; [they say] also that the Sultan [Jaqmaq] learned of this, and that he appointed a viceroy of Damascus and a viceroy of Aleppo, who are in their position at the present time, and that the Sultan kept silent concerning the subject. Some of the foremost men of the government said: "This is all idle talk; when the spring is over each of them will go his own way; they did all this only as a joke". This gained currency and

the matter was ended; it is something the like of which we have not heard in past ages.

Year 850 A.H.

The year 850 A.H. began with the rulers in the same positions as in the preceeding year excepting the Shāfi'ite Cadi, who was now al-Qāyātī; and the commander-in-chief, who was Īnāl; the grand executive secretary, who was Qānibāi al-Jarkasī. The viceroy of Alexandria, Tanam, who succeeded Alṭunbughā al-Laffāf; the viceroy of Gaza, Yalkhujā [min Māmish] who followed after Ṭūkh al- Abūbakrī.

March 29 Muḥarram 1 was a Tuesday.

April 28 Ṣafar 1 was a Thursday.

May 23 Monday, the 26th (of Ṣafar). (Ibrāhīm) as-Subainī was invested with the office of Shāfi'ite Cadi of Aleppo in place of Sirāj ad-Dīn al-Ḥimṣī because of the latter's removal.

June 30 Thursday (II Rabī') 4 (5). Muḥibb ad-Dīn ibn al-Ashqar was invested to remain in the office of controller of the army, because Burhān ad-Dīn ibn ad-Dairī had made a strong effort to secure this office and promised a large sum—about 8,000 dīnārs—which he would pay to the Sultan. The Sultan agreed and he (Ibn ad-Dairī) went up on this day to be appointed, but the agreement was broken and (Muḥibb ad-Dīn) put on the robe of continuance in office, then went down to his home in an immense cortège,

VIII, 21 and paid attention to no one.

I Jumādā 1 was a Tuesday (Monday). On this day Ibn ash-Shiḥna was invested with continuance in his various offices, as Cadi, confidential secretary, and controller of the army—all in Aleppo—after he had sent to the Sultan an amount of money and gifts too large to describe. This was displeasing to the Aleppans for he prolonged his stay among them and acted in these official positions with a display of respect.

July 29 Friday, the 4th (5th of I Jumādā), corresponding to (Coptic) Misrā 5. The Nile reached plenitude, and His Highness, Fakhr ad-Dīn, the Sultan's son, went down (from the Citadel) and opened the Cairo Canal Dam as usual. By Shihāb ad-Dīn ibn Faḍl Allāh al-'Umarī are two verses (in Rajaz meter; rhyming words: *bāhir* (in first half verse), *an-naḍir*, *wal-khaḍir*.)

II Jumādā and Rajab: nothing happened in these two months.

Oct. 22 Sha'bān 1 was a Saturday.

Nov. 5 Saturday, (Sha'bān) 15. The prisoners who were in the Maqshara (Prison) conspired together, killed the jailer, and all escaped.

Nov. 8 Tuesday (Sha'bān) 18. A number of the Sultan's purchase of mamlūks went down (to Cairo), pursued Zain ad-Dīn, the executive secretary, and beat him with maces until he almost perished; had he not entered the house of Ṭūkh min Timrāz, an emir of the first class, he would have lost his life.

Ramaḍān. Nothing happened in this month.

Dec. 20 Shawwāl 1 was a Tuesday.

Dec. 23 Friday, the 4th. Badr ad-Dīn ibn at-Tanasī, the Mālikite Cadi, was removed from office because he had kept a man for a long time in prison; then he was invested to remain in office.

*VIII, 22 *Dhu l-Qa'da 1 was a Thursday (Wednesday).

Jan. 18 Saturday, the 3rd (4th). Ismā'īl ibn 'Umar al-Hawwārī arrived
A.D. 1447 in Cairo from Upper Egypt to acknowledge his loyalty (to the
Jan. 21 Sultan of Egypt), and the Sultan invested him with a robe of acceptance, and gave him a horse with a gold saddle and brocaded saddle cloth.

Jan. 28 Saturday, the 10th (11th). Jānibak al-Yashbakī, an emir of the third class and a head of guards, was appointed governor of Cairo after the removal of Manṣūr ibn aṭ-Ṭablāwī because of (the Sultan's) dislike of the latter.

Jan. 31 Tuesday, the 13th (14th). Jānibak, mentioned above, was invested and appointed one of the chamberlains, in addition to his office as governor.

Feb. 17 Dhu l-Ḥijja 1 was a Friday.

Feb. 20 Monday, the 4th (of Dhul-Ḥijja). (Ṣadr ad-Dīn) Ibn an-Nuwairī was appointed Shāfi'ite Cadi of Aleppo after the removal of (Burhān ad-Dīn Ibrāhīm ibn 'Umar] as-Sūbīni.

March 11 Saturday, the 23rd [of Dhu l-Ḥijja]. The announcer of the pilgrimage Aḥmad ibn Jānibak arrived [at Cairo] and announced peace and security [of the pilgrims].

Year 851 A.H.

The year began with the Caliph and Cadis the same as before, except the Shāfi'ite Cadi, who was 'Alam ad-Dīn Ṣāliḥ al-Bulqīnī, appointed on the first day [of the year] in place of Shaikh of Islam Ibn Ḥajar because of the latter's removal; [the rest of the executive officials were:] commander in chief of the armies, Īnāl [al-'Alā'ī an-Nāṣirī]; the emir of arms, Timrāz al-Qirmishī aẓ-Ẓāhirī; the emir of the council, Jarbāsh Qāshuq; the emir of the horse, Qarājā al-Ḥasanī; the grand chamberlain, Tanbak al-Bardbakī; the chief head of guards, Tamurbāi at-Tamurbughāwī; the executive secretary, Qānibāi al-Jarkasī. The remainder of the emirs of the first class were: His Highness Fakhr ad-Dīn 'Uthmān, son of the Sultan;
VIII, 23 Asanbughā aṭ-Ṭayyārī; Ṭūkh min Timrāz an-Nāṣirī Bīnī Bāziq; Shihāb ad-Dīn Aḥmad ibn 'Alī ibn Īnāl; Alṭunbughā al-Mu'allim [al-Yalbughāwī], and emir of eighty horsemen. Other officials were:

second emir of horse, Jarbāsh Kurd; second head of guards, Jānibak al-Qirmānī aẓ-Ẓāhirī; second executive secretary, Daulāt Bāi al-Maḥmūdī al-Mu'ayyadī; second chamberlain, Nūkār an-Nāṣirī with a weak emirate of the third class, a man of no consequence; superintendent of the buttery, Yūnus as-Saifī Āqbāi; warden of the armory, Taghrī Birmish as-Saifī Yashbak ibn Uzdamur; viceroy of the citadel, Taghrī Birmish al-Faqīh; treasurer, Qarājā aẓ-Ẓāhirī Jaqmaq; chief eunuch of the palace, Fīrūz an-Naurūzī ar-Rūmī; commander of the Sultan's mamlūks, 'Abd al-Laṭīf al-Manjakī al-'Uthmānī; his deputy, Jauhar an-Naurūzī.

Bureau Officials: confidential secretary, Kamāl ad-Dīn ibn al-Bārizī; deputy confidential secretary, Mu'īn ad-Dīn 'Abd al-Laṭīf ibn al-'Ajamī; controller of the army, Muḥibb ad-Dīn (Muḥammad ibn 'Uthmān) ibn al-Ashqar; vizier, Ṣāḥib Karīm ad-Dīn 'Abd al-Karīm ibn Kātib al-Manākh; controller of privy funds, Jamāl ad-Dīn Yūsuf ibn Kātib Jakam; major domo, Zain ad-Dīn Yaḥyā al-Ashqar, relative of Ibn Abi l-Faraj; controller of the stables, Burhān ad-Dīn (Ibrāhīm) ibn ad-Dairī al-Ḥanafī; scribe of the bureau of mamlūks, Faraj ibn an-Naḥḥāl.

Viceroys of Syria and elsewhere: Damascus, Julbān, emir of the horse; Aleppo, Qānibāi al-Bahlawān an-Nāṣirī; Ṭarābulus, Barsbāi min Ḥamza an-Nāṣirī; Ḥamā, Yashbak aṣ-Ṣūfī; Ṣafad, Baighūt al-A'raj; Gaza, Yashbak al-Ḥamzāwī; Malaṭyā, Qānṣūh an-Naurūzī; al-Karak, Ḥājj Īnāl (min Yashbak) al-Jakamī; Alexandria, Tanam min 'Abd ar-Razzāq, the market inspector. These are those who are referred to each as "king of the emirs" (malik al-umarā'). As for the remainder of the viceroys of the fortresses and cities, they are numerous.

Rulers of (other) regions: Mecca, Sharīf Barakāt ibn Ḥasan ibn 'Ajlān; Medīna, City of the Prophet (upon whose inhabitants be
VIII, 24 the best of prayer and peace!), Sharīf Umyān ibn Māni' ibn 'Alī al-Ḥusainī; al-Yanbu', Sharīf Hilmān [ibn Zubair ibn Nakhbār].

Ruler of Harāt and other Persian kingdoms: al-Qa'ān Mu'īn ad-Dīn Shāh Rukh ibn Tīmūrlank and a number of his sons and descendants over a number of kingdoms including the ruler of Samarqand and elsewhere, al-Qa'ān Saif ad-Dīn Ulūgh Bak ibn al-Qa'ān Mu'īn ad-Dīn Shāh Rukh, son of the tyrant Tīmūrlank; Adharbaijān and elsewhere of the kingdoms of 'Irāq, Jahān Shāh ibn Qarā Yūsuf ibn Qarā Muḥammad; rulers of Diyār Bakr, a number of the sons of Qarā Yuluk, the greatest of whom was the grandson of Qarā Yuluk, Jahān Kīr ibn 'Alī Bak ibn Qarā Yuluk.

The ruler of Burṣa (Brusa) in the land of Rūm [Byzantium] and elsewhere, Khawandkhār Murād Bak ibn Muḥammad Abī Yazīd ibn Murād ibn 'Uthmān; ruler of Lāranda and elsewhere in the land of Qaramān, Ṣārim ad-Dīn Ibrāhīm ibn Qaramān; on another side of the land of Rūm [Byzantium], Isfandiyār; viceroy of Abulustān, Sulaimān ibn Nāṣir ad-Dīn Bak Muḥammad ibn Dulghādir. Ruler of Tūnis, Bajāya and the rest of the land of Ifrīqiya, Sultan Abū Amr 'Uthmān ibn Abī 'Abd Allāh Muḥammad ibn Abī Fāris 'Abd al-'Azīz ibn Abi l-'Abbās Aḥmad al-Ḥafṣī al-Maghribī; the rest of the land of al-Maghrib was in the hands of a number of kings explanation of whose names would be too tedious.

March 19 Muḥarram 1 was a Saturday (Sunday, March 19, A.D. 1447).

April 18 Ṣafar 1 was a Monday (Tuesday, April 18).

April 19 Wednesday, Ṣafar 3 (2). Aitmish min Azūbāi al-Mu'ayyadī, the chief steward, died, as will be related

April 24 Monday, Ṣafar 8 (7). Khawājā Badr ad-Dīn Ḥasan ibn Shams ad-Dīn Muḥammad al-Muzalliq ad-Dimashqī was appointed controller of the army of Damascus after the removal of Mūsā ibn Jamāl ad-Dīn al-Karakī and his departure again to the controllership of the army of Ṭarābulus.

May 25 Thursday, (I Rabī') 10 (9). Alṭunbughā, mamlūk of Ṭarabāi,
VIII, 25 was appointed chamberlain of Gaza for a sum of money which he offered for the removal of Ibn Buwali (spelled with vowel *u* to *b*, and *l* with vowel *ī*).

May 26 Friday, I Rabī' 11 [10]. Baibars ibn Baqar was reappointed Shaikh of the Arabs in the eastern district of the province of Cairo, and Ibn Jammāz was also reappointed to his shaikhdom.

June 16 II Rabī' 1 was a Thursday [Friday].

June 20 Tuesday, the 6th [5th], corresponding to Ba'ūna 26, one of the Coptic months. The low level of the Nile was taken and the basis was found to be 11 cubits, 12 fingers, something not witnessed before.

Aug. 1 Tuesday, the 17th [18th of I Jumādā], corresponding to Misrā 7, one of the Coptic months. The Nile reached plenitude, and His Highness Fakhr ad-Dīn, son of the Sultan, rode down, opened the dam and did all that was customary. In the verses by Ibn Nubāta [on this occasion, are these, in kāmil meter, with rhyming words: *fil-bilādī, dhī ayādī*].

Jan. 11 Thursday, [Dhu l-Qa'da] 4. [Walī ad Dīn Muḥammad ibn
A.D. 1148 Aḥmad ibn Yūsuf] as-Safṭī was appointed lecturer of the Ṣāliḥīya College Mosque and its controller, in place of the Shaikh of Islām Ibn Ḥajar.

Jan. 18 Thursday, the 11th [of Dhu l-Qa'da]. Taqī ad-Dīn [Abū Bakr] ibn Qāḍī Shuhba, the jurist of Syria, died suddenly in Damascus, and was buried in the morning.

Feb. 7 Dhu l-Ḥijja 1 was a Tuesday [Wednesday]. On this day Ṣafī
VIII, 26 ad-Dīn Jauhar ibn 'Abd Allāh al-Manjakī al-Ḥabashī, commander of the mamlūks and builder of the College Mosque opposite the Citadel, died suddenly, and was buried the next day.

Feb. 8 Thursday, the 3rd [2nd]. An individual of the inhabitants of Marṣafā came [to Cairo] and reported that he had seen the new moon on the eve of Tuesday. Men were much confused, for the sky had been completely overcast from the beginning of Tuesday eve until Thursday. Walī ad-Dīn as-Safṭī, the Shāfi'ite Cadi, wished to accept [the statement of] the observer in that he [as-Safṭī] would decree of his own knowledge the fixation of the month. Then one of his deputies informed him that he [the informant] was a false witness and that he, while he was deputy cadi in Marṣafa, had prevented him from giving testimony. As-Safṭī rebuked the deputy who gave him this information, and ordered that another like him be examined; he came and confirmed on Friday the fourth of the month, that the first of it [i.e., of Dhu l-Ḥijja] was Tuesday; [this was] out of fear lest the Festival of the Sacrifices [i.e., Dhu l-Ḥijja 10] should fall on a Friday, for the Egyptians drew omens of misfortune from the delivery of two sermons on one day.

Feb. 15 Thursday, the 10th [9th of Dhu l-Ḥijja]. Cadi Walī ad-Dīn as-Safṭī was invested with a Kāmilīya robe and a sable fur following the sermon of the Festival.

Feb. 22 Thursday, the 17th [16th]. Shihāb ad-Dīn Aḥmad ibn Naurūz al-Khiḍrī, superintendent of flocks in Syria, came to Cairo.

Feb. 28 Wednesday, the 23rd [22nd]. Uzbak as-Sāqī aẓ-Ẓāhirī, herald of the Pilgrimage, arrived and reported the safety and security [of the Pilgrims].

March 2 Saturday, the 26th [25th]. Cadi 'Izz ad-Dīn 'Abd ar-Raḥīm Ibn al-Furāt al-Ḥanafī died.

Wednesday, the last day [of Dhu l-Ḥijja]. Walī ad-Dīn as-Safṭī took to the Sultan, from the storehouse of the [Manṣūrī] Hospital, 10,000 dīnārs which he displayed to him; the Sultan thanked him
VIII, 27 for this.

Year 852 A.H.

The year began with all its government officials as they had been in the preceeding year.

March 7 Muḥarram 1 was a Thursday.

On Muḥarram 1 the report arrived of a great battle in Upper Egypt between Ismā'īl al-Hawwārī and the Banū Bukairān, the Lahyān, and others, in which battle were killed Muḥammad, brother of Ismā'īl, just mentioned, and others among his relatives and followers; then victory over them came to him and he killed about 500. The messenger was invested.

March 9 Saturday, the 3rd. The banishment to Qūṣ of the Ḥanbalite Cadi of Aleppo, Majd ad-Dīn Sālim, was ordered because the Mālikite Cadi in Aleppo was indebted to him; he wished to demand payment from him and the debtor asked that he [the creditor] relinquish some of the debt but he refused.

March 10 Sunday, the 4th. The gift of Zain ad-Dīn, the major-domo, for the Sultan arrived; the number of horses was 600 mares of which 60 were with ornamented saddles, three with gold horse cloths with brocaded collars and brocaded housings; and 30 with saddles of Bulgarian leather.

March 21 Thursday eve, the 15th [of Muḥarram]. Shaikh Burhān ad-Dīn Ibrāhīm ibn Khiḍr al-'Uthmānī died.

Wednesday, [Muḥarram] 21. Shaikh Shihāb ad-Dīn [Aḥmad ibn 'Uthmān] ar-Rīshī died.

April 5 Ṣafar 1 was a Friday in accordance with observation.

April 8 Monday, the 4th [3rd]. The heads of the men, the rebellious Arabs, arrived at Cairo, sent by the inspector-governor of Bahnasāwīya.

On the same day Tamurbāi at-Tamurbughāwī, chief head of guards, set out for Upper Egypt in company with Ismā'īl ibn 'Umar al-Hawwārī and 200 Sultan's mamlūks to fight the rebellious Hawwāra Arabs.

*VIII, 28
April 12 Friday,* the 8th [7th]. The report arrived that there had occurred between Tanam min 'Abd ar-Razzāq al-Mu'ayyadī, viceroy of Aleppo and the people of Aleppo, dissension and some fighting and hurling of stones. Bardbak at-Tājī was designated to investigate and confirm this report.

Tuesday eve the 12th [11th]. Aqṭuwah al-Mūsāwī aẓ-Ẓāhirī died, and prayer was said for him on the next day.

April 20 Saturday, the 16th [15th]. Julbān, viceroy of Damascus, arrived at Cairo and encamped on the Race Course.

April 22 Sunday eve, the 17th [16th]. Shaikh Zain ad-Dīn 'Abd ar-Raḥman as-Sandabīsī died.

April 30 Tuesday, the 26th [25th]. Sharīf Umyān, emir of Medīna, city of the Prophet, arrived at Cairo and went up to the Sultan, who descended to him from the dais, walked some short steps to him, and showed him honor, investing him [with a robe] and giving him a horse to ride from the Sultan's court.

Ṣafar, toward end. Asanbāi aẓ-Ẓāhirī, the warden of the armory, died and his fief was divided.

May 5 I Rabī' 1 was a Sunday.

[Tuesday, I Rabī' 3]. A report arrived from Tamurbāi that the Arabs in Southern Egypt had become subservient to the Sultan and put on his robes, and that the rebellious Arabs and their followers had fled and left the land.

Wednesday, the 4th. A reply was written [to Tamurbāi] that he and those with him should remain [in Southern Egypt] until he would receive permission to come [to Cairo].

May 12 Sunday eve, the 8th. The Raḥba Prison was broken into, and some of the prisoners fled, while some were caught and others escaped.

May 26 Sunday, the 22nd. Sa'd ad-Dīn Ibn ad-Dairī removed himself
VIII, 29 as Ḥanafite Cadi, then was restored on Monday, the 23rd.

June 4 II Rabī' 1 was a Monday [Tuesday]. Sunqur aẓ-Ẓāhirī Jaqmaq, the treasurer, was ordered banished to Ṭarābulus.

June 7 [II Rabī' 4] Tamurbāi, chief head of guards, arrived from Upper Egypt on summons and was invested [with a robe]. With him arrived the Emir Ismā'īl ibn 'Umar al-Hawwārī.

June 8 Saturday, the 6th [5th]. The Sultan ordered that Shams ad-Dīn [Muḥammad al-Ḥanafī ar-Rūmī] the Scribe be brought to the Ṣāliḥīya [College Mosque] in order that among other charges there might be brought against him the charge that he had maligned the Imām ash-Shāfi'ī. So he was brought there and the complaint lodged against him before Cadi Nāṣir ad-Dīn Ibn al-Mukhallaṭa al-Mālikī and there was confirmed before him what he had attributed to al-Ghazzālī. It was decreed that Shams ad-Dīn be taken to prison on foot and with uncovered head.

June 10 Monday, the 8th [7th]. [Ibn Ḥajar] put on the robe of reappointment and went down to the Ṣālihīya as before, and Īnal al-'Alā'ī, the commander-in-chief was given an outer robe with gold border with the reappointment as controller of the Manṣūrī Hospital. Also Shams ad-Dīn the Scribe was taken from prison and ordered banished to Aleppo.

June 11 Tuesday, the 9th [8th]. Sharaf ad-Dīn al-Munāwī put on a robe with his appointment as lecturer in the Shāfi'ite Mosque; he went there, lectured, then returned.

On the same day Shams ad-Dīn the Scribe was returned to prison because he was charged with maligning the Prophet (blessing and peace be upon Him!)

June 12 Wednesday, the 10th [9th]. Nāṣir ad-Dīn Muḥammad ibn Abi l-Faraj, the adjuntant of the army, went down to the prison, took Shams ad-Dīn the Scribe and went to the Mu'ayyadī Mosque so that the Ḥanafite Cadi Ibn ad-Dairī might hear the charge against him.

*VIII, 30 * Thursday, II Rabī' 11 [10]. Zain ad-Dīn [Yaḥyā], the major-
June 13 domo, was invested with a Kāmilīya robe with a sable as before, and 'Abd Allāh, the inspector-general of the Eastern District, was invested with the outer robe of his continuance in office.

June 15 Saturday, the 13th [12th]. Shams ad-Dīn the Scribe was ordered to go to his dwelling and remain there ten days during which he should prepare himself to go to Jerusalem to stay there.

June 16 Sunday, the 14th [13th]. Shihāb ad-Dīn Aḥmad the inspector-governor was ordered to go to Damascus to remain there. And a report was received that there had occurred between the viceroy of Jerusalem Timrāz al-Baktamurī al-Mu'ayyadī al-Muṣārī' and its controller, Amīn ad-Dīn 'Abd ar-Raḥmān ibn ad-Dairī, a 'great battle with weapons of war on account of Abū Tibr; the order went out to investigate this report at the hand of Saif ad-Dīn Kizil al-Qardamī.

June 18 Tuesday, the 16th [15th]. Shaikh 'Alī the market-inspector put on the green kāmilī robe of his maintenance in the office of market inspector.

Also [on the 16th] Shams ad-Dīn the Scribe was ordered to stay in Cairo and there was returned to him whatever had been in his possession.

June 19 Wednesday, the 17th [16th]. Shaikh of Islām Ibn Ḥajar went up to Cairo wearing a robe of continuance in office; he was accompanied by the Cadis and jurists.

June 20 Thursday, the 18th [17th]. Daulāt Bāi al-Maḥmūdī al-Mu'ayyadī, the second executive secretary, put on a kāmilīya robe with a sable fur as controller of the Baibarsīya College Mosque.

June 21 Friday, the 19th [18th]. Shihāb ad-Dīn Aḥmad ibn Qāḍī Shams ad-Dīn al-Qāyātī came [to the Baibarsīya] as its Shaikh; and on the same day Aḥmad, the inspector-governor, set out for Damascus.

June 23 Sunday, the 21st [20th]. Ṣāḥib Karīm ad-Dīn 'Abd al-Karīm ibn Kātib al-Manākh died, removed from office.

June 24 [II Rabī' 22 (21)]. Asanbughā al-Kalbakī was designated [to become viceroy of Jerusalem]; then this was changed because of Asanbughā's lack of fitness for the office, and a delay was fixed until Kizil, who had gone to investigate the report [concerning the battle between the viceroy and the controller of Jerusalem] should come [to Cairo].

*VIII, 31 June 28 * Friday, the 26th [25th]. Sūrbāi the Circassian concubine of the Sultan, died in Būlāq after she had remained there some days for recuperation when her sickness was prolonged; she was buried the next day.

July 1 Monday, the 29th [28th]. Jānim the executive secretary known as Khamsumi'a [Five Hundred] came to Cairo from his journey to Damascus.

July 3 I Jumādā 1 was a Wednesday.

July 4 Thursday, I Jumādā 2. The Shaikh of Islām Ibn Ḥajar was appointed lecturer of Shāfi'ite law and controller of pious trust foundations in the Ṣāliḥīya Mosque.

July 6 Saturday, I Jumādā 4. A council was convened before the Sultan and a complaint lodged against Badr ad-Dīn Maḥmūd ibn 'Ubaid Allāh al-Ḥanafī, that a certain individual read in the "Riyāḍ aṣ-Ṣāliḥīn" of an-Nawawī in connection with the subject of the mission of the Prophet and its manner, and that he asked "is this correct or not correct?" The case was referred to the Ḥanbalite [Cadi], and four men, including his ward Aḥmad ibn Faraj ibn Uzdamur, and Taghrī Birmish, warden of the armory, testified against him; he reaffirmed his faith and his life was spared.

On the same day the Grand Princess Mughul, daughter of al-Bārizī, was transferred from the Grand Hall to the Barbarīya Hall and the Sultan reported that he had divorced her about eight months ago and mentioned that she was the cause of the death of Sūrbāi by sorcery—[I say] God save her from that.

July 7 Sunday, [I Jumādā] 5. Kamāl ad-Dīn ibn al-Bārizī, the confidential secretary, was appointed controller of the Jamālīya Monastery as a partner to Sāra, daughter of the founder, in place of as-Safṭī.

July 11 Thursday, [I Jumādā] 9. Abū 'Abd Allāh al-Baidamurī al-Maghribī was appointed Mālikite Cadi in Damascus in place of Shihāb ad-Dīn [Aḥmad] at-Tilimsānī.

July 13 Saturday, [I Jumādā] 11. A report arrived [in Cairo] of the death of Shāhīn as-Saifī Ṭūghān (the executive secretary), viceroy of the citadel of Damascus; 'Alā ad-Dīn 'Alī ibn 'Abd Allāh, the
VIII, 32 warden of the armory, was designated to guard his possessions.

Also Kizil al-Qardamī, who had gone [to Jerusalem] to investigate the matter concerning its viceroy and its controller, returned with a document concerning what had occurred between the two.

July 20 Saturday [I Jumādā] 18. Amīn ad-Din 'Abd ar-Raḥmān ibn ad-Dairī, who had been removed [as viceroy of Jerusalem], arrived [in Cairo], while Timrāz [al-Baktamurī] remained in Jerusalem as its viceroy.

July 25 Thursday, [I Jumādā] 23. Shams ad-Dīn al-Ḥamawī the Scribe was appointed controller of Jerusalem in place of Cadi Amīn ad-Dīn 'Abd ar-Raḥmān ibn ad-Dairī.

July 31 Wednesday [I Jumādā] 27, corresponding to Misrā 6, one of the Coptic months. The Nile reached plenitude and His Highness, Fakhr ad-Dīn, the Sultan's son, went down, opened the dam after performing the accustomed routine. By Burhān ad-Dīn al-Qīrāṭi are these lines [in Sarī' meter, with rhyme words: *khālā* and *ḥālā*].

Aug. 1 Thursday, end of I Jumādā. Yalbughā al-Jārkasī, an emir of the third class, put on the robe of the viceregency of the Damietta fortress in place of Baisaq al-Yashbakī.

Aug. 2 II Jumādā 1 was a Friday.

Aug. 7 Wednesday, II Jumādā 6, Jānibak aẓ-Ẓāhirī, superintendent [viceroy] of Judda, arrived in Cairo.

Aug. 8 Thursday, II Jumādā 7, Nāṣir ad-Dīn Muḥammad ibn Amīr 'Alī, the Sultan's boon companion, died.

Aug. 22 Thursday, II Jumādā 21. Taqī ad-Dīn Muḥammad ibn 'Izz ad-Dīn aṣ-Ṣairafī put on [the robe of] the Shāfi'ite judiciary in Ṭarābulus.

Also on this day Muḥibb ad-Dīn Ibn ash-Shiḥna, Cadi of Aleppo,
Aug. 24 arrived at Cairo. Then on Saturday, the 23rd, he went up to the Sultan, who invested him with a Kāmilīya robe with a sable fur.

And on this day Amīn ad-Dīn Ibn ad-Dairī also was invested with a Kāmilīya robe with a sable fur.

*VIII, 33 * On the same day, too, the Sultan's attitude changed toward an individual known as Asad ad-Dīn the Alchemist, because of the prolongation of his work without any apparent result; and the Sultan ordered the release and deliverance from him of the merchant Ibn Shams. In the account of the alchemist and Ibn Shams was the fact that the alchemist had swindled him [Ibn Shams] and taken considerable sums of money from him, and also had written against him a promissory note for 2,000 dīnārs. Then when they quarreled the alchemist demanded the money, and one of the mischief makers took him up to the Sultan and said of him that he practiced alchemy. The Sultan's greed was aroused; he demanded to hear what he had to say; immediately he made a decision concerning Ibn Shams, and was successful in having this decision accepted.

The affair of the alchemist with Ibn Shams is too long to explain; but when the Sultan heard the words of the alchemist and thought that he would be successful in the practice of alchemy he put Ibn Shams under guard until there had been taken from him for Asad ad-Dīn the sum which had been written and he vacated for him a place in which to practice alchemy. So he [the alchemist] began to exercise control over the Sultan and his followers after he exercised control over Ibn Shams. Included in his control was that he said: "Why do not the chief officials come to me in my place?" So the Sultan ordered them to go to him, and they all went to him and sat before him, while he addressed them with exceeding seriousness, speaking with them only by means of an interpreter. When he took from Ibn Shams the sum mentioned the report came to him that Ibn Shams had said: "Soon the falsehood of Asad ad-Dīn will become evident to the Sultan." Asad ad-Dīn said: "I shall do nothing until Ibn Shams is banished to Jerusalem". Then he [Ibn Shams] was banished to Jerusalem.

There had happened to him with Ibn Shams something resembling this story; namely, that the wife of Ibn Shams said to her husband: "By Allāh! this one lies; and if he knew the science
VIII, 34 of alchemy he would indeed be happy and rich without the need of help from any one." The words of the woman reached him and

he said to her husband: I will do nothing for you until you divorce her." But he hesitated to divorce his wife and she said to him: "Divorce me and do not leave any excuse for him." So he divorced her, and when Ibn Shams went to Jerusalem and this affair wearied the Sultan and he learned what Asad ad-Dīn had done with Ibn Shams he was certain that he had lied, that he could not do anything well, and he began to consider all his words.

Aug. 23 Friday, II Jumādā 22. The gate of Bashbāi Bridge looking upon Riṭlī lake was ordered closed, and the residents there were ordered to move from that region. The deputy of the governor went there with his police; much confusion and some plundering occurred among the men, and the furniture of the shops at the Bridge was destroyed.

Aug. 24 Saturday, the 23rd. Sitt al-Mulūk, daughter of aẓ-Ẓāhir Ṭaṭar and wife of Yashbak, the commander-in-chief, died and was buried in the morning.

Aug. 26 (II Jumādā 25.) A proclamation was issued concerning the inhabitants of the (Bashbāi) Bridge and the opening of its gate as usual. Likewise a proclamation was issued concerning copper coins, that the coin should be 36 (dirhams).

Aug. 29 Thursday, (II Jumada) 28. The sun was eclipsed from a little before noon until about 30 degrees after sunset, and prayer for the eclipse was recited in the Azhar Mosque.

Sept. 2 [Rajab 3]. In the afternoon Shaikh Zain ad-Dīn Riḍwān [ibn Muḥammad ibn Yūsuf al-'Uqbī], secretary of traditionists, died and was buried the next day.

Sept. 9 Monday, [Rajab 10]. The confidential secretary, Kamāl ad-Dīn Ibn al-Bārizī put on a Kāmilīya robe with a sable fur.

Sept. 13 Friday [Rajab 14]. The Princess, daughter of Jarbāsh, moved to the great Columned Hall [of the Sultan's Palace], taking the place of [Mughul], daughter of al-Bārizī.

Sept. 21 Saturday (Rajab) 22. The vizier Amīn ad-Dīn ibn al-Haiṣam
*VIII, 35 put on a *Kāmilīya robe with sable fur on account of supervision of the dikes; and Cadi Badr ad-Dīn ibn Qāḍī Ba'labakk put on the robe of the controller of the army of Ṣafad in place of Ibn al-Qaff.

Sept. 22 (Rajab 23). Asad ad-Dīn ad-Kīmāwī went up to the Sultan and mentioned that he was truthful in what he had claimed and that he would accomplish it quickly; the Sultan showed him honor, though by God (who is the only God) he was lying.

And on this day Zain ad-Dīn (Yaḥyā) put on a kāmilīya robe with sable fur.

Sept. 28 Saturday, (Rajab) 29. Abu l-Khair an-Naḥḥās was appointed controller of escheats attached to the vizierate.

Sept. 30 (Monday, Sha'bān 1). Shaikh Abu l-Fath ibn Wafā' died; prayer for him was said in 'Amr Mosque, and he was buried in his tomb in the Qarāfa Cemetery.

On the same day prayer was said for Burhān ad-Dīn al-'Uryānī in the Azhar Mosque; he had drowned at the end of Wednesday, Rajab 26 at Furanj Ferry, and his body had appeared on Tuesday at as-Samāsim near the Siryāqaus Monastery; it was buried there. Then his relatives went and brought it to Cairo, but it had become very inflated and its odor had changed (God have mercy on him).

Oct. 1 (Sha'bān 2). The office of controller of escheats attached to the vizierate was returned to the vizier, and similarly the controllership of water wheels, for both of them had been taken over by an-Naḥḥās.

Oct. 10 Thursday, Sha'bān 11. The Vizier put on a red satin kāmilīya with a sable fur, because of retaking the controllership of escheats and water wheels.

Oct. 13 Sunday (Sha'bān) 14. Aḥmad ibn Naurūz, superintendent of flocks, died; his fief was bestowed upon Aḥmad, the Sultan's son; and Qānim at-Tājir was appointed emir of the advance caravan in his place.

*VIII, 36 * Tuesday, (Sha'bān) 16. Shihāb ad-Dīn Aḥmad al-Madanī,
Oct. 16 who claimed that he was the agent of the Sultan, was beaten before the Mālikite Cadi in the Ṣāliḥīya College Mosque more than a hundred blows, a chain was placed upon his neck, and he was imprisoned in the Dailam prison. (This punishment) was because of the charge which he had brought against Shams ad-Dīn the Scribe but which had not been confirmed; (this charge) had been brought in the council of Cadi Nāṣir ad-Dīn ibn al-Mukkhal-liṭa in the presence of the Mālikite Cadi, as we have narrated, and your Lord does not oppress his servants!

And on this day a heavy rain fell with lightening which killed a trooper in the Qūṣūn Zarība on Arwā Island, known as Middle Island.

Oct. 18 Friday, [Sha'bān] 19. The Sultan put on his colored woolen garments—I mean his winter clothing—and similarly clothed the emirs as usual.

Oct. 20 Sunday, [Sha'bān] 21. A council was convened before the Sultan with the Shāfi'ite Cadi, 'Alā' ad-Dīn al-Qalqashandī, Sharaf ad-Dīn al-Munāwī, and some of a group of Shāfi'ites, on the subject of the preacher Jamāl ad-Dīn 'Abd Allāh ibn Jamā'a, shaikh of the Ṣalāḥīya in Jerusalem, because it was said that he was not fitted to teach, and because he had signed a number of erroneous legal opinions. The motive for calling this convention was Sirāj ad-Dīn al-Ḥimṣī, for he had requested that he [Ibn Jamā'a] be brought for him [al-Ḥimṣī] to examine. The Shāfi'ites and the preachers came, but al-Ḥimṣī delayed coming, so the Sultan became angry with him, and the position of preacher remained with Jamāl ad-Dīn Ibn Jamā'a, while al-Ḥimṣī was refused even the possibility of ascending to the Citadel.

Oct. 21 Monday, [Sha'bān] 22. The Sultan ordered that Ibn Nuwairī, Shāfi'ite Cadi in Aleppo before this date, be placed in irons and go to Aleppo to answer a charge brought against him by [Ḍiyā' ad-Dīn] ibn an-Naṣībī.

*VIII, 37 Oct. 24 * Thursday, [Sha'bān] 25. Badr ad-Dīn Ibn Qāḍī Ba'labakk, controller of the army of Ṣafad, was removed from office and Ibn al-Qaff was restored to it.

Oct. 27 Sunday, [Sha'bān] 28. Jamāl ad-Dīn Ibn Jamā'a, shaikh of the Ṣalāḥīya [College Mosque in Jerusalem], put on the robe of continuance of office, and on Tuesday, last day [of Sha'bān], departed for Jerusalem.

Oct. 29 Ramaḍān 1 was a Wednesday [Tuesday].

On this day Badr ad-Dīn Ḥasan ibn al-Muzalliq, controller of the army of Damascus, arrived in Cairo.

Nov. 2 Friday, [Ramaḍān] 3 [4]. Taghrī Birmish al-Faqīh died in Jerusalem of the plague while he was out of service.

Nov. 3 Saturday, Ramaḍān 4 [5]. The purchased mamlūks intended to inflict harm upon [Zain ad-Dīn] the major-domo and to rob his home. The major-domo became aware of this and remained in the Duhaisha; he did not go down to his house, but quickly sent, removed all that was in it, and closed its barricades. The Sultan then sent after a number of them [the mamlūks], including Qānṣūh, whom he struck with his poniard because there had occurred between him and the major-domo a quarrel on account of his peasants; but a reconciliation had then been concluded between them and he gave Qānṣūh a salārī with a sable fur—by the life of my grandfather how the times have declined! And when Qānṣūh put on the salārī he went to the purchased mamlūks to turn them away from the major-domo; but they cursed him and said: "We did this only for your sake". Then the major-domo went down accompanied by Qarājā the treasurer and others, until he came to his home.

Nov. 6 Tuesday, [Ramaḍān] 7 [8]. Zain ad-Dīn the major-domo went up and the Sultan invested him with a kāmilīya with a sable fur. As he went out he was told that the Sultan's mamlūks were waiting for him so he turned back, entered the vestibule of the Basin Hall [Baḥra] which is in the Royal Park of the Citadel. The Sultan sent after Uzbak the cupbearer and Asanbāi the cupbearer, ordered the two to go with him [the major-domo] until he should reach his home. But he refused to go with them out of fear of being killed, and he threw off the robe. Each of the two cupbearers mentioned

spoke with the purchased mamlūks and implored them that for
VIII, 38 their sake, they leave him [the major-domo] free today, and thereafter they might do whatever they desired. So they desisted from him [the major-domo] until he reached his home. On Thursday, the 9th (8th of Ramaḍān) the Sultan reviewed the purchased mamlūks, spoke to them about the major-domo, and placated them as much as he could.

Nov. 9 Saturday, the 11th (12th of Ramaḍān). Zain ad-Dīn (the major-domo) put on the kāmilīya, the robe of continuance in office, and returned to their former holders a number of fiefs which had entered into the Sultan's special bureau.

Nov. 16 Saturday, the 18th (19th of Ramaḍān). The report arrived of the death of Shihāb ad-Dīn Aḥmad, inspector-governor of the Gharbīya, who was in Damascus at the time.

Nov. 18 Monday (Ramaḍān 21). A number of the people of Bilbais came (to Cairo) and reported that they had fasted on Tuesday, and that Taghrī Birdī al-Qillāwī, the inspector-governor, had claimed that he had seen the new moon on Tuesday eve in Jīza; it was mentioned of another that he also had seen it.

In the last decade of the month the Sultan's sister arrived from the land of Circassia.

Nov. 28 Shawwāl 1 was a Tuesday.

Dec. 12 Thursday, (Shawwāl) 15. Tanbak the grand chamberlain put on the robe of inspector of dikes; and Abu l-Yumn an-Nuwairī was appointed Shāfi'ite Cadi in Mecca in place of Abū as-Sa'ādāt ibn Ẓuhaira, while Abū 'Abd Allāh at-Turaikī was removed from the Malikite cadiship of Damascus, and Sālim was appointed in his place.

Dec. 16 Monday, (Shawwāl) 19. The caravan of the mamlūks rode from Pilgrim Lake; the two shaikhs Amīn ad-Dīn Yaḥya ibn al-Aqṣarā'ī, shaikh of the Ashrafīya, and 'Aḍud ad-Dīn 'Abd ar-Raḥmān ibn aṣ-Ṣīrāmī, accompanied it.

Dec. 18 Wednesday, (Shawwāl) 21. The advance caravan set out, and the litter caravan followed it the next day, after a heavy rain had fallen upon them.

Dec. 21 Saturday, Shawwāl 24, Shaikh 'Alī, the market-inspector put on the robe of continuance in office, a kāmilīya with a sable fur.

*VIII, 39 * Saturday, Dhu l-Qa'da 15 [16]. The Sultan became disaffected
Jan. 11 toward the negroes who were in Cairo because some of them had
1449 A.D. attacked the women's bath in Munyat 'Aqaba, and one of the jurists had issued a judicial decree that they were combatants; he [the Sultan] then acted decisively and ordered their seizure and imprisonment.

Jan. 13 Monday [Dhu l-Qa'da] 17 [18]. The Sultan ordered Rājiḥ ibn ar-Rifā'ī and his adherents that they should not perform in their chapels any thing forbidden such as playing on flute or tambourine, in accord with a royal rescript requested by the sons of Shaikh 'Abd al-Qādir al-Kīlānī, who claimed that they had lodged a complaint against Rājiḥ with the Ḥanbalite Cadi and that he had given this decision against them.

Jan. 26 Eve of [Sunday, Dhu l-Ḥijja 1]. The master-engineer Muḥammad ibn Ḥusain aṭ-Ṭūlūnī, the Sultan's architect-engineer, died and prayer over him was said in the Sultan's presence in the Mu'minī Oratory.

Jan. 27 Monday, [Dhu l-Ḥijja] 2. 'Alam ad-Dīn [Ṣāliḥ] al-Bulqīnī put on a kāmilīya with a sable fur, the robe of continuance as Shāfi'ite Cadi.

Jan. 28 Tuesday, the 3rd. The Sharīf Aḥmad an-Nu'mānī died. On the same day the plague appeared in Egypt.

Feb. 15 Saturday, [Dhu l-Ḥijja] the 21st. The order was given to seize Aṣad ad-Dīn the Alchemist; the second executive secretary Daulāt Bāi, the governor Jānibak, and the adjutant of the army, went down from the Citadel, surrounded his house and seized his property. They found 242 dīnārs belonging to him, a small number of Persian and Turkish books on subjects pertaining to alchemy; four carats of diamonds, some garments, a box containing some herbs, paste, and nutmeg. He was taken up to the Sultan, a chain and fetters were placed upon his neck, and he was put in the Tower. The feelings of the Sultan toward the market-inspector
VIII, 40 changed and he placed him under guard because he was the one who had taken this liar to the Sultan, recommended him to him and strenghtened his determination to draw him near to himself.

Feb. 16 Sunday, Dhu l-Ḥijja 22. The announcer of the Pilgrimage, 'Alā' ad-Dīn 'Alī ibn 'Abd Allāh the merchant and warden of the armory, arrived and reported that the halt had been observed on Monday at 'Arafāt and that prices were moderate.

On the same day a council was assembled before the Sultan on account of Asad ad-Dīn the Alchemist, and Mālikite Cadi Badr ad-Dīn at-Tanasī was of the opinion that he should be imprisoned; so Asad ad-Dīn was paraded around and heralded, then imprisoned in the Maqshara.

Feb. 20 Thursday, the 26th [of Dhu l-Ḥijja]. Timrāz al-Baktamurī al-Mu'ayyadī al-Muṣāri', former viceroy of Jerusalem, arrived in Cairo, and was ordered to remain in Cairo out of service.

Eve of Saturday, the 28th. The Shaikh of Islām [Chief Cadi Shihāb ad-Dīn Aḥmad] Ibn Ḥajar [al-'Asqalānī] died.

Feb. 22 Saturday [Dhu l-Ḥijja 28]. 'Alā' ad-Dīn al-Qalqashandī was appointed to the lectureship on apostolic traditions in the Ibn Ṭūlūn Mosque; Jalāl ad-Dīn al-Maḥallī was appointed to the lectureship in law in the Mu'ayyad Mosque; 'Alam ad-Dīn al-

Bulqīnī to the lectureship and controllership in the Ṣālaḥīya and Shams ad-Dīn ibn Ḥassān to the lectureship in traditions in the Baibarsīya Tomb [Qubba]—all of these appointments were in place of Ibn Ḥajar because of his death.

Feb. 22 On this day also a council of scholars and cadis was assembled before the Sultan on the subject of Asad ad-Dīn the Alchemist, against whom several charges were brought; one of these was that he was an unbeliever and that he denied the Prophet's mission. The Mālikite Cadi said: "My school accepts his repentance," and sent to him one of the Mālikite scholars named Shams ad-Dīn ad-Daisaṭī al-Mālikī, who said: "(according to our) school he is an atheist." He was assisted in this verdict by Abu l-Faḍl al-Maghribī, Shaikh Aḥmad al-Adabī, and others; Abu l-Faḍl expanded the statement on this subject and said: "If it is permitted him to

VIII, 41 issue a judgment concerning him, let it be done"; the Mālikite and the Sultan gave permission, and all of them went down to the Ṣalāhīya; but nothing was done on this day.

Year 853 A.H.

The year began with officials as before except those we mentioned at the date (of change).

March 4 Tuesday, (Muḥarram) 9. Timrāz, former viceroy of Jerusalem, complained to the Sultan against Amīn ad-Dīn ʿAbd ar-Raḥmān ibn ad-Dairī and charged that he had caused in Jerusalem an uprising as a result of which fighting had occurred and one of the mamlūks of Timrāz had been killed; that Ibn Dairī had proclaimed the closing of the Aqṣā Mosque and the waging of holy war on Timrāz; and that he (Timrāz) was an infidel. The Sultan became enraged at this and ordered that a chain be placed upon Ibn Dairī's neck and he be sent to Maqshara Prison. So the chain was placed on his neck and he was taken away; but then intercession was made for him and the chain was taken from his neck at the gate of the Mosque which is in the Citadel; both he and his rival were ordered to be carried to the Mālikite Cadi, and so they were both taken to him.

March 6 [Muḥarram 11.] Asad ad-Dīn the Alchemist was executed decause his atheism had been confirmed before Shams ad-Dīn Muḥammad ad-Daisaṭī the Mālikite; then afterwards ad-Daisaṭī had added in writing that there was confirmed before him the fact that Asad ad-Dīn was a lying infidel. I say: "His execution was one of the greatest benefits for Islam, for his career with the Persians had for reasons which are mixed been evil in those lands;" and also there happened to him with Ulūgh Bak ibn Shāh Rukh events in which was involved the loss of his own life, but his fate actually occurred only in Egypt. His death was grievous to many men among those who did not know the truth about him but thought that only after his execution occurred the plague, dearth, and failure of the Nile flood, while these are in reality misfortunes, not events like those suggested; and all which you see comes through predestined fate.

March 6 [Muḥarram 11]. The register of deaths passed 100 per day.

March 9 Sunday, [Muḥarram] 14. Shihāb ad-Dīn al-Hītī, one of the students, died.

*VIII, 42 March 10 * Monday [Muḥarram] 15. Shihāb ad-Dīn al-Masṭīhī, one of the deputy cadis, died. The registry of deaths on this day reached 116; at the Oratory of Succar Gate alone the number was more than 100, but the registry on the days of the plague were not reliable.

March 11 Tuesday [Muḥarram] 16. The registry [of deaths] reached 114, and on the following day, 182.

March 14 Friday, the 19th [of Muḥarram]. The caravan of mamlūks sojourning [in Mecca] arrived in Cairo.

March 15 Saturday, the 20th [of Muḥarram]. The advance caravan entered Cairo, its emir being Qānim at-Tājir; then on the next day the litter-caravan arrived, its emir being Sawinjbughā al-Yūnusī an-Nāṣirī, both of whom were emirs of the third class.

March 26 Ṣafar 1 was a Wednesday.

On this day the plague became severe in Egypt; the number who died in it was more than about 1,000; for there is no reliability in the death statistics of the bureau, because when the plague became severe most men did not register their dead but took coffins of the pious foundation. For this reason during the plague the statistics are unreliable.

March 26 And on this Wednesday Prince Aḥmad, the Sultan's son, died.

March 27 Thursday, the 2nd [of Ṣafar]. 'Alā' ad-Dīn al-Kirmanī, shaikh of the Sa'īd as-Su'adā' Monastery, died.

March 31 Monday, the 6th [of Ṣafar]. The Sharīf Ḥasan ibn 'Alī who had been removed as syndic of the Prophet's descendants, died; also Burhān ad-Dīn Ibrāhīm ibn Ẓahīr, controller of the stables, died, and he was buried the next day.

[March 26] And on the 1st of this month there had died in Damietta the Sharīf 'Alī ibn Ḥasan ibn 'Ajlān, who had been deposed as emir of Mecca; but the news of his death arrived [in Cairo] on Friday, the 10th [of Ṣafar].

VIII, 43 April 4 On the Friday mentioned died Timrāz, emir of arms, and he was buried the next day, as will be noted in the necrologies.

April 5 Saturday, the 11th [of Ṣafar]. A number of important personages died, namely, the Sultan's nine year old daughter, the twin of Aḥmad, mentioned shortly before; and the daughter of the Caliph

Mustakfī Billāh; also Nāṣir ad-Dīn Muḥammad ibn Ṭūghān al-Ḥasanī, the executive secretary in the reign of an-Nāṣir Mu' ayyad; and the treasurer Kamāl ad-Dīn ibn al-Bārizī. This day was a frightful day, one in which the important officials were in doubt as to which funeral they should attend.

April 7 Monday, the 13th [of Ṣafar]. Badr ad-Dīn at-Tanasī, Mālikite Cadi in Egypt, died.

April 9 Wednesday, the 15th [of Ṣafar]. Uzbak as-Sāqī aẓ-Ẓāhirī Jaqmaq died, and the Sultan was present at the prayer over him; also Īnāl al-Yashbakī [died] as will be noted in the necrologies.

April 11 Friday, the 17th [of Ṣafar]. There died in Cairo each of these two: Walī ad-Dīn Ibn al-Yumn Muḥammad ibn Qāsim and Ismā'īl ibn 'Umar al-Hawwārī.

April 12 Saturday, the 18th [of Ṣafar]. There died Prince Muḥammad, five year old son of the Sultan by a slave girl; Qarā Qujā al-Ḥasanī, grand emir of the horse, died that same day, as did also his son, close to twenty years of age; the burial of the father was delayed so that the funeral of the two might be held together on the morrow; great grief was expressed for each of them.

April 13 Sunday [the 19th of Ṣafar]. Jānim aẓ-Ẓāhirī Jaqmaq, the executive secretary known as Jānim Five Hundred, died; also Princess Fāṭima, five year old daughter of the Sultan by a slave girl, died.

*VIII, 44
April 14 * Monday, the 20th [of Ṣafar]. The plague apparently abated—rather, it had abated several days before this; but while the diminution of the plague increased on this day, at the same time very many deaths occurred—we ask God [to avert death] upon Islam.

April 14 Eve of Monday, the 20th [of Ṣafar]. The Sharīf Abū l-Qāsam ibn Ḥasan ibn 'Ajlān, who had previously been removed from the emirate of Mecca, died; and the Sultan's sister, who had come to him from Circassia in the early days of the past year or the year before that, likewise died.

April 15 Tuesday, the 21st [of Ṣafar]. The wife of the Sultan, Princess Nafīsa, daughter of Nāṣir ad-Dīn Bak ibn Dulghādir, died, and the Sultan attended the prayer over her.

April 16 Wednesday, the 22nd [of Ṣafar]. Prince Muḥammad, six year old son of the Sultan, also by a slave-girl, died; likewise Bakhtak an-Nāṣirī, an emir of the third class, died.

April 20 Sunday, the 26th [of Ṣafar]. Saif ad-Dīn Bardbak al-Khāṣṣakī aẓ-Ẓāhirī Jaqmaq, known as Bardbak Twelve, died; also there died the Lady Irdbāi the Circassian wife of Timrāz, emir of arms, who had died shortly before; and the credited Shaikh Shams ad-Dīn Muḥammad ibn 'Abd ar-Raḥmān ibn Sulṭān also died.

April 22 [Tuesday, the 28th of Ṣafar]. Shams ad-Dīn Muḥammad ibn Āmir, one of the deputy Mālikite Cadis in Alexandria, was appointed [Cadi of Egypt] in place of Walī ad-Dīn.

And the Sultan ordered the banishment of Qushtam an-Nāṣirī, inspector-governor of Buḥaira, to Jerusalem and the banishment of Īnāl as-Sāqī aẓ-Ẓāhirī, known as Khawand, to Ṭarābulus because he had struck Faraj, scribe of the bureau of Mamlūks, a painful blow.

April 23 Wednesday, the 29th. Tamurbāi at-Tamurbughāwi, chief head of guards died; likewise the wife of Kamāl ad-Dīn ibn al-Bārizī, the daughter of Emir Nāṣir ad-Dīn Muḥammad ibn al-ʿAṭṭār; she was one of the best of women in her time in religion, in worship and in piety, God have mercy on her.

*VIII, 45 * Muḥammad, son of Zain ad-Dīn ʿAbd al-Bāṣit [also died this day] at approximately 20 years of age; he was the third son of his father who died in this plague.

April 25 Friday, the 2nd [of I Rabīʿ]. An expedition set out for Buḥaira under command of Jarbāsh Kurd accompanied by five other emirs.

And on this day died Lady Sāra, daughter of commander-in-chief Āqbughā at-Timrāzī and wife of His Highness Nāsir ad-Dīn Muḥammad ibn aẓ-Ẓāhir Jaqmaq; her mother was my sister. The Sultan prayed over her the next day in the Mu'nimī Oratory—God have mercy on her.

April 28 [Monday, I Rabīʿ 5]. The fief of Tamurbāi was bestowed on Baighūt, viceroy of Ḥamā, and he was ordered by letter to come to Cairo; but this was changed some days later.

April 29 Tuesday, the 6th [of I Rabīʿ]. Zain ad-Dīn ʿAbd ar-Raḥmān ibn ʿAbd ar-Raḥīm, son of the chamberlain, died.

May 5 Monday, the 12th [of I Rabīʿ] Timrāz was removed as viceroy of Jerusalem and Khushqadam al-ʿAbd ar-Raḥmānī was restored to its viceregency.

May 6 Tuesday, the 13th [of I Rabīʿ]. Shihāb ad-Dīn Aḥmad ibn Badr ad-Dīn ibn Muzhir died.

During these days the plague was light in Cairo, but increased in the suburbs.

May 7 Wednesday, the 14th [of I Rabīʿ]. Aidakī aẓ-Ẓāhirī Jaqmaq, the executive secretary, died.

May 12 Monday, the 19th [of I Rabīʿ]. Jānibak, known as Shaikh al-Bajmaqdār, was banished to Aleppo.

May 29 Thursday, the 7th [6th of II Rabīʿ]. Kamāl ad-Dīn Ibn al-Bārizī, the confidential secretary, put on a kāmilīya with a sable fur, the robe of continuance in office, and he was given a horse with a gold saddle and brocaded horsing.

June 9 Monday, the 17th [of II Rabīʿ]. The report arrived of the death of Khushqadam, viceroy of Jerusalem; Mubārak Shāh as-Saifī
VIII, 46 Sūdūn min ʿAbd ar-Raḥmān, one of the emirs of Damascus, was appointed in his place.

And on the same day 'Alā' ad-Dīn ['Alī ibn Muḥammad] ibn Aqbars put on a kāmilīya, the robe of continuance in the office of market inspector, on the payment of a sum of money which he paid to the treasury. And Fāris as-Saifī Jār Quṭlū, who had before this been removed from Qaṭyā, was appointed commander in chief of Gaza in place of Timrāz al-Ashrafī because of the latter's arrest.

June 18 Wednesday, the 27th [26th of II Rabī']. A council of the Shāfi'ite Cadi and a number of Shāfi'ite jurists met on the subject of Ibn Aqbars.

In this month there came reports from the region of Aleppo that its people were in great alarm on account of Jahān Kīr ibn 'Alī Bak ibn Qarā Yuluk; there was much discussion among the people on the subject and the men spoke about a journey by the Sultan to Syria.

June 25 [Wednesday I Jumādā 4]. Wheat sold at 300 [dirhams] per irdabb, beans at about the same, and barley at a dīnār, while the price of flour rose above 100 per baṭṭa.

July 9 Wednesday, the 18th [of I Jumādā]. The Sultan ordered the seizure and banishment of the former market inspector Shaikh 'Alī. He was placed under guard until the end of the day; then both he and his deputy, 'Izz ad-Dīn 'Abd al-'Azīz al-Anbābī, after an understanding had been effected, were released.

July 20 [I Jumādā 29. Al-Bulqīnī was removed from office] because Ibn Isḥāq, one of his deputies in Old Cairo, had given a decree concerning the marriage of a woman whose husband had died after he had divorced her in his fatal sickness, and had communicated to 'Alā' ad-Dīn Ibn Aqbars that she was separated from him after proof had been established before him that he had died while she was still married to him. Then another line of proof was presented to Ibn Isḥāq and it as said that it was exactly the same as the evidence just mentioned, namely, evidence that he had divorced her before his death; and he [Ibn Isḥāq] had decreed that she was still legally married to him. A report of this reached the
VIII, 47 Sultan, who summoned Ibn Isḥāq, gave him a painful beating, and imprisoned him in the Maqshara; then his master [al-Bulqīnī] was deposed, and it was rumored that Jalāl ad-Dīn al-Maḥallī was appointed, but he said: "I shall accept only under certain conditions, including this, that I shall not have jurisdiction over the pious foundations and not be appointed as Cadi of the open country"; thus his refusal of the position became clear; thereupon the officials of the government spoke about returning the Cadi [al-Bulqīnī], who accepted and was invested on the morrow with a robe of remaining in office.

July 22 II Jumādā 1 was a Tuesday. On this day Cadi 'Alam ad-Dīn put on the robe of continuance in office as noted before.

The month began with prices a little lower, wheat selling at 290 per irdabb, beans at 240, and barley at 160—and this was despite the fact that the level of the Nile this year was a number of fingers less than it had been on the same date in the previous year.

July 24 Thursday, the 3rd [of II Jumādā]. The Sultan designated Timrāz min Baktamur al-Mu'ayyadī al-Muṣāri', who had previously been removed from the viceregency of Jerusalem, to journey to Southern Egypt accompanied by a number of Sultan's mamlūks.

Aug. 7 Thursday, the 17th [of II Jumādā]. The Sultan sent the second executive secretary Tamurbughā to go to Buḥaira Province bearing a written order to the emirs who were on an expedition there to free the Muḥārib Arabs who had been seized. This was after the Sultan had become angry at the emirs because during the absence of the emirs, the Arabs had gone to the Sultan, who had granted them security and bestowed robes upon them; then when they [the Arabs] went to Buḥaira and confronted the emirs they [the emirs] had seized them because they considered that seizing them was their best policy.

Aug. 15 Friday, the 25th [of II Jumādā]. Tamurbughā came back from Buḥaira Province after releasing those on account of whom he had gone there.

Aug. 14–18 [II Jumādā 24–28. Wheat sold at 400 dirhams per irdabb]; the men crowded against the stores of the bakers and the populace
VIII, 48 stole bread from the shops. Conditions became severe until a baṭṭa of flour sold at 135 per irdabb, wheat at about 400—the matter belonged to God before and afterward. The Thursday mentioned was [Coptic] Misrā 21.

Aug. 17 Sunday, the 27th [of II Jumādā]. The Sultan's brother came from the land of Circassia; he had come to Cairo before this on another occasion in the reign of al-Ashraf; he was ugly in appearance, but his soul was even uglier than his appearance.

Aug. 18 Monday, the 28th. Qarājā al-'Umarī, former governor of Cairo, came from Damascus.

Aug. 19 A rise of four fingers in the Nile was proclaimed, so two fingers of the deficiency were made up, and six fingers to fulfilment remained on Tuesday, corresponding to [Coptic] Misrā 26. This is something the like of which only rarely had been seen before.

Aug. 20 Wednesday, the last [of II Jumādā], corresponding to Misrā 27. The Nile reached 16 cubits and two fingers of the 17th cubit. The people were extremely happy at this. Fakhr ad-Dīn, the Sultan's son, went down, crossed the Nile, perfumed the Nilometer, then returned and opened the Canal of the Dam as usual. It was a day witnessed by many; the grandson of al-Malik al-Ḥāfiẓ did well when he recited on this subject [two verses in kāmil meter, with rhyming words: *masrūrā*; *maksūrā*].

*VIII, 49 * Rajab 1 was a Thursday [Wednesday].

Aug. 21 On this day the Nile rose five fingers, and the joy of the men increased even more than yesterday; and Jānibak, superintendent of Judda, sent his gift [to the Sultan]; Abu l-Khair an-Naḥḥās had aroused the Sultan's anger against him with statements most of which were untruthful and the Sultan ordered him placed under guard; his case eventuated the payment of over 30,000 dīnārs.

Aug. 21 Friday, the 2nd [3rd of Rajab]. A rise of eight fingers in the level of the Nile was announced and with them 15 fingers of the 17th cubit [i.e., 16 cubits 15 fingers], were attained—thanks be to God; but despite this the price of wheat was more than 400 [dirhams per irdabb]; and a baṭṭa of flour was as high as 150.

Aug. 30 Saturday, the 10th [11th of Rajab]. The Sultan ordered the banishment of Cadi 'Alam ad-Dīn al-Bulqīnī to Jerusalem; but one of the prominent members of the government spoke to him about the Cadi, and the Sultan ordered him to remain in his house out of service; then afterwards he ordered again that he be placed under guard and be banished to Ṭarsūs; but when intercession was again made in behalf of the Cadi the Sultan ordered him to go to Jerusalem, and he took to adjusting his affairs. One of the officials in the course of some business between us at that time said to me: "Have you heard that the Chief Cadi has been banished to Ṭarsūs?" I said to him: "We know only that they are confined in the Maqshara with the criminals". I meant by this as-Safṭi; the bystanders laughed, and I said: "In this time of ours it is not unknown what is done with Cadis and others, for the Sultan (God aid him) makes himself and the four Cadis a measure for the lowest ranks or the purchased mamlūks or others like them whom he wishes to praise and would say: "This one is better
*VIII, 50 than I" or "better than the four Cadis"; and *perchance this would happen in their presence, and in that case what the Sultan did concerning them or others would not remain generally unknown.

Sept. 1 Monday, the 12th [13th of Rajab]. Qarājā al-'Umarī set out for Jerusalem because of his appointment there; for a few days before this he had been appointed viceroy of Jerusalem, by request, in place of Mubārak Shāh as-Saifī Sūdūn min 'Abd ar-Raḥmān.

And Sūdūn al-Muḥammadī Atmakjī, second emir of the horse, died.

Then 'Alā' ad-Dīn al-Qalqashandī was ordered to be appointed lecturer in the Khashshabīya [Chapel] in place of 'Alam ad-Dīn; he accepted while in the council, then, after he had gone down [from the Citadel] he resigned, because he knew that the lectureship had been in the possession of the Bulqīnī family for about 60 years.

Then on the 15th [16th of Rajab] 'Alam ad-Dīn al-Bulqīnī was ordered not to journey to Jerusalem but to remain at home out of service.

Sept. 9 [Rajab 20 (21)]. The reason [for the Sultan's order to Damascus to flog and imprison Zain ad-Dīn ibn al-Kuwaiz, the Sultan's major-domo there] was that when he reached there the Sultan sent an order that he should sit above its emirs except its commander in chief Khairbak al-Mu'ayyadī; this displeased the emirs, and Julbān, the viceroy of Damascus, wrote to the Sultan on the subject. The Sultan disapproved what had occurred, rebuked Kamāl ad-Dīn the confidential secretary and cursed him roundly; it appears that Zain ad-Dīn in carrying out the Sultan's order, had gone to excess as suited his own feelings—but God knows [whether this is true].

Sept. 13 Saturday, the 24th [25th of Rajab]. The report came [to Cairo] that Qarājā, viceroy of Jerusalem on his way to that city, had been intercepted by Baibars ibn Baqar, shaikh of the Arabs in
*VIII, 51 Sharqīya, who *had fled from the Halbā Suwaid, rebel Arabs; Qarājā aided Baibars and fought together with him. The two won a victory after a great battle in which they killed a large number and captured about eighty, it was said. When the Sultan received the report he sent Jānibak, superintendent of Judda to bring the captives to Cairo after nailing them upon camels.

Sept. 15 [Rajab 26 (27)]. Sunqur al-'Ā'iq came from Buḥaira, and was invested with the appointment as third emir of the horse, which office had been designated for him during his absence, as has been noted before.

Sept. 21 [Sha'bān 2 (3)]. The populace rejoiced at the appointment of him [Zain ad-Dīn Yaḥyā to administer the office of market inspector] because yesterday, the day on which there happened to Abu l-Khair what we have narrated, he ordered a proclamation to be made that on Saturday he would sell wheat at a dīnār after [it had been sold] at 500 [dirhams]. Then when he went down from the Citadel and began to administer the office of market inspector he sent and opened his granary on the Būlāq shore and sold wheat from it; but he falsified regarding the prices, for he sold at 500 dirhams. However, the absence of all compulsion proved to be advantageous to the men, for Ibn Iskandar had placed restrictions on selling the wheat, releasing only a portion of it to the buyer. As a result (so it was said) he would sell wheat at a certain price, then sell it at another price higher than the first until some man bought wheat without his permission and he would beat him, parade him publicly, and proclaim: "This is the punishment, and the least punishment, of one who buys wheat. I say: [He took] also other measures of this kind".

Sept. 22 Monday, the 3rd [4th of Sha'bān]. Khairbak al-Mu'ayyadī, an emir of the third class, arrived in Cairo from Upper Egypt with those who had gone with him.

Nūkār the chamberlain from Aleppo arrived also.

*VIII, 52 * Thursday, the 7th. Jānibak, superintendent of Judda, and
Sept. 25 'Abd Allāh, inspector-governor of Sharqīya District, came to Cairo, with the Arabs who had been seized, approximately eighty in number, nailed to camels in a non-fatal manner; the Sultan ordered them to be imprisoned in the Maqshara; and when I saw them, I asked one whose name was Damurdāsh and who had before this date been inspector of Sharqīya: "Who are these?", and he answered: "Sellers of dates in Qaṭyā."

Sept. 24 The final height of the Nile this year was three fingers of the 19th cubit; this was on Wednesday, Sha'bān 6, corresponding to Coptic Tūt 27.

Oct. 16 Thursday, the 28th [of Sha'bān]. The report came from Damascus of the death of Baisaq al-Yashbakī, viceroy of the citadel of Damascus.

Oct. 18 Ramaḍan 1 was a Sunday [Saturday].

Ramaḍān began with the people in distress and affliction because of the excess in prices of all food, especially wheat, for it was sold at 600, beans at 500, barley at 400, flour at about 200 the baṭṭa; the price of everything was double what it had been before; meat could be found only with great effort. This was while the corresponding Coptic month was Bābā, and the people were still far from the harvest.

Oct. 24 Friday, [Ramaḍān 6], corresponding to Bābā 26. The Sultan put on colored woolen garments for the winter, and clothed the emirs of the first class as usual.

Oct. 25 Saturday, the 7th [8th of Ramaḍān]. Chief Cadi Sa'd ad-Dīn Ibn ad-Dairī al-Ḥanafī deposed himself on account of the bath of as-Safṭī and the earlier judgment concerning it which had involved him. Qāsim the inspector-governor, owner of the bath, produced the decree of one of the Cadis of the Rīf District which nullified the judgment of Sa'd ad-Dīn, while the Sultan showed an inclination favoring this Cadi; then when this became evident to Cadi Sa'd ad-Dīn he resigned from the office of Cadi and in-
VIII, 53 sisted on refusing the office; and even when he was requested to return to it, he refused.

Nov. 1 Saturday, the 14th [15th of Ramaḍān]. The Cadi [Sa'd ad-Dīn ibn ad-Dairī], after repeated refusals, was restored to the office of Cadi, as he had been before.

Nov. 2 [On Ramaḍān 16] Asanbughā aṭ-Ṭayyārī, chief head of guards, and Jarbāsh Kurd, went to Buḥaira to fight the rebellious Arabs.

Nov. 4 Tuesday, the 17th [18th of Ramaḍān]. A report of the death of Shams ad-Dīn al-Ḥamawī, controller of Jerusalem, arrived at Cairo.

Nov. 17 Shawwāl 1 was a Tuesday [Monday].

Nov. 22 Saturday, the 5th [6th of Shawwāl]. Jamāl ad-Dīn Yūsuf al-Bā'ūnī was removed from the office of Shāfi'ite Cadi of Damascus, and the Sultan wrote to an-Nuwairī, Cadi of Ṭarābulus, ordering the office to him; but Kamāl ad-Dīn, the confidential secretary, confronted him and said: "This is an ignorant man, he will not be fit to be Cadi of Damascus." The Sultan replied: "The Cadi of Aleppo?" Kamāl ad-Dīn repeated what he had said, that both of them were unworthy to be Cadis of Damascus. The Sultan said: "We shall appoint Shaikh 'Alā' ad-Dīn al-Qalqashandī." Jamāl ad-Dīn, controller of privy funds, said: "He is not willing." He [the Sultan] said to him: "We shall force it upon him", and was gruff in saying this. Then when Kamāl ad-Dīn went down [from the Citadel] he questioned 'Alā' ad-Dīn on the subject, and he refused absolutely. This answer was returned to the Sultan and he ordered the appointment of Sirāj ad-Dīn al-Ḥimsī, who was at that time Shaikh of the Jerusalem Ṣalāḥīya [College Mosque].

Nov. 29 Saturday, the 12th [13th of Shawwāl]. The Sultan seized Najm ad-Dīn Ayyūb ibn Badr ad-Dīn Ḥasan ibn Nāṣir Muḥammad, known as Ibn Bishāra, commander of the Clansmen [i.e., Druze] in the country of Sidon, and imprisoned him in the Tower of the Citadel.

VIII, 54 In this year the Pilgrimage was performed by Tūkh Bīnī Bāzīq, and by Shihāb ad-Dīn Aḥmad ibn Īnāl al-'Alā'ī. Also Fairūz set out, while there were various sayings about his two offices, and his power was on the wane, because it was customary that Naqāda, which was a part of the pious foundations of the servitors in holy Medīna should be under the control of the chief eunuch of the palace. And when, before these days, he had told the Sultan of the failure of its income in this year, the Sultan had said to him: "Make the expenditures from what you now have, then take from the future income." Then he commanded Abu l-Khair an-Naḥḥās to administer the office. Abu l-Khair said: "It is a proviso that the controllership of the office should belong to one who is a eunuch of the palace." The Sultan replied: "I have appointed you eunuch of the palace." Abu l-Khair indicated with his hand that he had a penis. The Sultan said: "And if they were two I still have appointed you." So Abu l-Khair was compelled to go down and from his own possessions tie up the burden, which amounted to about 3,000 dīnārs. And this was the purpose of the Sultan, even if the world should be turned upside down. If Abu l-Khair at that time had deserved the office of chief eunuch of the Palace, he had it.

Dec. 15 Monday, the 28th [of Shawwāl]. Asanbughā aṭ-Ṭayyārī, chief head of guards, and Jarbāsh Kurd, arrived at Cairo from the Buḥaira expedition.

Also Ibn 'Amir was removed from the office of Cadi of Alexandria in favor of a person known as al-Maḥallī, a Shāfi'ite by
VIII, 55 school, whereas it was customary that the office should be held by a Mālikite, but the Sultan broke the custom with great benefit to it.

Also Yashbak min Jānibak al-Mu'ayyadī aṣ-Ṣūfī was removed from the viceregency of Ṭarābulus because of the complaint of its inhabitants concerning his tyranny and evil conduct; then on the next day he was restored to the office.

Dec. 16 Dhu l-Qa'da 1 was a Wednesday [Tuesday].

Dec. 20 Saturday, the 4th [5th of Dhu l-Qa'da]. Yashbak aṣ-Ṣūfī was again removed from the office of cadi of Ṭarābulus, then restored to it, also again; there were several statements concerning his restoration.

Dec. 29 Monday, the 13th [14th of Dhu l-Qa'da]. Jamāl ad-Dīn al-Bā'ūnī was restored to the Shāfi'ite Cadiship of Damascus.

Jan. 1 Thursday, the 16th [17th of Dhu l-Qa'da]. The Sultan invested
A.D. 1450 Emir Ḥasan Bak ibn Sālim ad-Dūkārī with the viceregency of Ḥimṣ after the removal of Bardbak as-Saifī Sūdūn min 'Abd ar-Raḥmān.

Also Sharāf ad-Dīn Yaḥyā ibn al-'Aṭṭār died, and was buried the next day.

Jan. 15 Dhu l-Ḥijja 1 was a Thursday.

Jan. 16 Tuesday, the 2nd [of Dhu l-Ḥijja]. The Sultan contracted a marriage with the daughter of Kurtbāi, emir of Circassia, who had come previously to Cairo with his just mentioned daughter, when they both became Muslims and the father was circumcized and, as was said, made good his Mohammedanism. The Sultan slept with her that same night and ended her virginity. He had bestowed on his son Fakhr ad-Dīn 'Uthmān a slave girl, and he also ended her virginity that night; when the good news was announced to the Sultan he presented the announcer 200 dīnārs because of his joy over his son.

Jan. 17 Saturday, the 3rd [of Dhu l-Ḥijja]. 'Abd al 'Azīz ibn Muḥammad aṣ-Ṣughaiyir, an emir of the horse, was appointed one of the chamberlains in Cairo after he had made a gift of a number of horses.

[Dhu l-Ḥijja 8]. Shihāb ad-Dīn [Aḥmad ibn] az-Zahrī was ordered to be removed from the Shāfi'ite Cadiship of Ṭarābulus. Burhān ad-Dīn as-Sūbīnī was appointed in his place and was ordered to investigate the case of Yashbak aṣ-Ṣūfī, who had been removed from its viceregency.

And on the same day it was ordered to seize Qarājā al-'Umarī, viceroy of Jerusalem, and for Qarājā to go to Damascus out of service. Also Mubārak Shāh al-'Abd ar-Raḥmānī was restored to the
VIII, 56 viceregency of Jerusalem, and 'Allān Jullaq was restored to his chamberlainship [in Aleppo] at the intercession of the confidential secretary Ibn al-Bārizī, for he informed the Sultan that the letters which had come from 'Allān contained the statement that the disagreement which had occurred between him and the viceroy was the result only of his putting an end to the wrong doings in Aleppo and his command to do the right there. It was only because the Sultan heard this [explanation] that he restored him to office.

Jan. 28 Wednesday, the 14th [of Dhu l-Ḥijja]. A number of the people of Ma'arra came before the Sultan complaining against both Ṣārim ad-Dīn Ibrāhīm ibn Baighūt, viceroy of Ḥamā, and Ibn al-'Ajīl, and reported about both ugly things which necessitated the Sultan's disaffection toward them. So he sent Saif ad-Dīn Jānim aẓ-Ẓāhirī to Ḥamā to summon each of the two with a
Jan. 30 chain on his neck. He [Jānim] set out on Friday after the prayer. Every one thought that Baighūt would revolt and not send his son in this manner.

On this day [Dhu l-Ḥijja 14] Badr ad-Dīn Ḥasan ibn al-Muzalliq, controller of the army of Damascus, arrived in Cairo from the territory of Sidon, after investigating the matter of Najm ad-Dīn Ayyūb ibn Bishāra, who had before this been arrested; he brought along a number of letters containing severe charges concerning the person mentioned; among them was that he had married eight women, that he had with his own hand killed a number of people and ordered the killing of twenty-seven others, had during his administration of about four years gotten possession of 217,400 dīnārs, and other charges of this kind too long to explain.

Feb. 5 Thursday, the 22nd [of Dhu l-Ḥijja]. Qushtum an-Nāṣirī, who had before this come from Jerusalem, was invested with the appointment as inspector-governor of Northern Egypt (as he had been before) after the removal of Muḥammad aṣ-Ṣughaiyir.

*VIII, 57 Feb. 7 * Saturday, the 24th. The mamlūk of Qānibāi al-Ḥamzāwī, viceroy of Aleppo, and the mamlūk of 'Allān, its chamberlain, stood before the Sultan and debated, each one speaking on behalf of his master; the Sultan favored the viceroy.

And on this day [Dhu l-Ḥijja 24] the announcer of the Pilgrimage [Aidakī al-Ashrafī] arrived at Cairo and reported the death of the Sharīf Sirāj ad-Dīn 'Abd al-Laṭīf, Ḥanbalite Cadi of Mecca, and the death of the Shāfi'ite Cadi there, the preacher Abu l-Yumn an-Nuwairī. He reported also the safety of the pilgrims and the increasing cheapness of prices. This was unusual at this time because prices were high in Egypt; for in the preceding year wheat was at 120 [dirhams] per irdabb, beans at 100, and a baṭṭa of fine flour at 140; at the same time a baṭṭa of flour in Mecca sold at 10 dīnārs; threshed beans two waibas per dīnār, while this year conditions were the opposite; prices in Cairo were high, for an irdabb of wheat was at about 300 [dirhams], beans at 500; a baṭṭa of flour at 250, and scarce—rather it could not be found except with excessive difficulty, and at the same time a load of flour at Mecca was sold at the same price as in the year before, while beans sold at each four waibas for a dīnār. The general thought, however, was that prices would run otherwise than this [in Mecca, contrasted with Cairo].

Feb. 9 [Dhu l-Ḥijja 25]. It was ordered that three Arabic shaikhs in Buḥaira Province should be halved at the waist, and they were immediately cut in two. They were Ismā'īl ibn Zā'id, Raḥḥāb and Shaqar, and were in the prison in the Citadel. Furthermore, the emirate of Jānibak, who had been transferred to the chamberlainship of Damascus (an emirate of the first class there), was given to Bardbak al-'Ajamī, who had before this been removed from the viceregency of Ḥamā and was now staying in Damietta out of service.

*VIII, 58 * Similarly [in this year] occurred the completion of the renovation of the Ibn Qā'imāz Fountain outside Cairo; and Jamāl ad-Dīn, the controller of privy funds, began digging a well which was to be a water source for the Pilgrims at the station of al-Buwaib, the second of the stations of the Pilgrimage from Cairo.

Feb. 14

Year 854 A.H.

This year began with the following individuals in the respective offices: Caliph, Mustakfī Billāh Abu r-Rabī' Sulaimān; Sultan, aẓ-Ẓāhir Abū Sa'īd Jaqmaq; Cadis: Shāfi'ite, al-Munāwī; Ḥanafite, Ibn ad-Dairī; Mālikite, as-Sinbaṭi; Ḥanbalite, Badr ad-Dīn al-Baghdādī, who was in the Ḥijāz; grand emir [commander-in-chief], Īnāl an-Nāṣirī; emir of arms, Jarbāsh Qāshūq, who likewise was in the Ḥijāz; emir of the council, Tanam al-Mu'ayyadī; grand emir of the horse, Qānibāi al-Jarkasī; grand chamberlain, Tanbak al-Bardbakī; chief head of guards, Asanbughā aṭ-Ṭayyārī; grand executive secretary, Daulāt Bāi al-Maḥmūdī.

Emirs of the first class: His Highness Fakhr ad-Dīn 'Uthmān, son of the Sultan; Ṭūkh min Timrāz an-Nāṣirī; Shihāb ad-Dīn

Aḥmad ibn 'Alī ibn Īnāl; Alṭunbughā al-Laffāf aẓ-Ẓahirī; and Jarbāsh Kurd. Superintendent of the buttery, Yūnus as-Saifī Āqbāi, viceroy of Damascus; warden of the armory, Taghrī Birmish as-Saifī Yashbak ibn Uzdamur, both of whom were emirs of the second class.

Treasurer, Qarājā aẓ-Ẓahirī; viceroy of the Citadel, Yūnus al-'Alā'ī an-Naṣirī, both of whom were emirs of the third class.

Chief eunuch of the palace and treasurer, the eunuch Fīrūz
VIII, 59 an-Naurūzī, who was emir of the litter caravan this year; commander of the mamlūks, Jauhar an-Naurūzī; deputy commander of the Mamlūks, Marjān al-'Ādilī al-Maḥmūdī.

Bureau officials: confidential secretary, Kamāl ad-Dīn Ibn al-Bārizī; controller of the army, Mūḥibb ad-Dīn Ibn al-Ashqar; vizier, Amīn ad-Dīn [Ibrāhīm] ibn al-Haiṣam; Major-domo Zain ad-Dīn Yaḥyā Qarīb Ibn Abi l-Faraj; controller of privy funds, Jamāl ad-Dīn Ibn Kātib Jakam.

Kings of neighboring countries: Mecca, Sharīf Barakāt ibn Ḥasan ibn 'Ajlān; Medīna, Sharīf Amyān ibn Māni' ibn 'Alī al-Ḥusainī; al-Yanbu', Sharīf Hilmān.

Viceroys of Syria; Damascus, Julbān, emir of the horse; Aleppo, Qānibāi al-Ḥamzāwī; Ṭarābulus, Yashbak an-Naurūzī (he had not up to the present entered Ṭarābulus); Ḥamā, Baighūt al-A'raj al-Mu'ayyadī; Ṣafad, Yashbak al-Ḥamzāwī; Gaza, Khairbak an-Naurūzī; al-Karak, Ḥājj Īnāl al-Jakamī; Jerusalem, Mubārak Shāh al-'Abd ar-Raḥmānī (he was until the present in Damascus); Malaṭya, Jānibak al-Jakamī; Alexandria, Barsbāi al-Bajāsī.

Kingdoms of the Persians and Jaghatai: Lord of Samargand and other Persian Kingdoms, Ulūgh Bak ibn Shāh Rukh ibn Tīmūr Lank, who ruled the land after the death of his father Shāh Rukh and exiled the sons of his brother Bāi Sunqur to the ends of Persia; these sons of Bāi Sunqur were 'Alā' ad-Daula, Bābur, and Muḥammad, the last named of whom, Muḥammad, took possession of part of the country from the Persians and settled in it at a distance from Ulūgh Bak, while 'Alā' ad-Daula took refuge in a fortress with his paternal grandmother, Kahr Shāh Khātūn, who was also the mother of Ulūgh Bak.

Lord of Tabrīz, Baghdād, as-Sulṭānīya, and other cities, Jahān Shāh ibn Qarā Yūsuf ibn Qarā Muḥammad at-Turkumānī.

Diyār Bakr was with the sons of Qarā Yuluk, the greatest of whom was Jahān Kīr ibn 'Alī Bak ibn Qarā Yuluk.

*VIII, 60 * Lord of Burṣā [Brusa], Adrianople, and other cities of Asia Minor, Khundkār Murād Bak ibn Muḥammad Kirishjī ibn Yildarīm Bāyazīd ibn Murād ibn Arin Khān ibn Urdan 'Alī ibn 'Uthmān ibn Sulaimān ibn 'Uthmān.

Part of Asia Minor: Isfandiyār ibn Abū Yazīd and in Qaramān Ibrāhīm ibn Qaramān.

Viceroy of Abulustain: Sulaimān ibn Nāṣir ad-Dīn Bak Muḥammad ibn Dulghādir.

Kingdoms of the West: Lord of Tūnis, Bijāya, and remainder of Ifrīqiya, Sultan Abū 'Amr ibn Abī 'Abd Allāh Muḥammad ibn Abī Fāris 'Abd al-'Azīz ibn Abi l-'Abbās Aḥmad al-Ḥafṣī al-Maghribī.

Kingdoms of the Europeans: Seventeen kings, to mention whom would take too long.

Kingdom of Abyssinia: the infidel Khaṭṭī and his adversary Sa'd ad-Dīn, lord of Jabart (may God aid him!).

This year began with the price [of commodities] in it [as follows]: an irdabb of wheat at 800 dirhams or less; barley, the same and hard to find; a baṭṭa of fine flour at 270 or less; a pound of bread at 6, but plentiful at this time while at an earlier date it was scarce and hard to find, but then became plentiful in the shops, thank God.

Feb. 14 [Saturday, Muḥarram 1]. The Sultan invested Muḥammad ibn Tūqān ibn Muḥammad with the appointment as Emir of the Āl Faḍl Arabs, in place of his nephew al-'Ajal ibn Qurqmās ibn Ḥasan ibn Nu'air because of the latter's removal.

*VIII, 61 Feb. 23 * Monday, the 10th [of Muḥarram]. Āqbirdī as-Sāqī aẓ-Ẓāhiri, viceroy of the citadel of Aleppo, arrived in Cairo, stood before the Sultan, then alighted in the Race Course.

Feb. 24 Tuesday, the 11th [of Muḥarram]. Zain ad-Dīn 'Abd al-Bāsiṭ arrived from the holy Ḥijāz and ascended to the Citadel, kissed the ground, was invested with a white woolen kāmilīya robe with a sable fur and sable lining, and then went down to his home accompanied by the chief men of the government. He had come to Cairo by dromedary, having left behind in al-'Aqaba Jarbāsh Qāshuq and the Ḥanbalite Cadi; all of them had left Mecca after finishing the rites there and had not gone to holy Medīna because they had visited it on their way to Mecca; for this reason they reached Cairo on this [early] date.

March 6 Friday, the 21st [of Muḥarram]. A caravan of many pilgrim mamlūks and others, who had been sojourning in Mecca, arrived in Cairo.

March 7 Saturday, the 22nd [of Muḥarram], Jānim aẓ-Ẓāhirī the cupbearer came from Ḥamā accompanied by Ibrāhīm ibn Baighūt al-Mu'ayyadī al-A'raj, viceroy of Ḥamā and Ibn al-'Ujail, shaikh of Ma'arra, both of whom were in irons; Jānim stood them before the Sultan, and immediately their accusors appeared. The Sultan listened to the letter which Jānim had brought from the viceroy of Ḥamā, then ordered the imprisonment of the two in the Tower of the Citadel, without having heard the charge of the complainants; rather the feelings of the complainants were satisfied by his statement: "Your opponents have appeared"; then he immediately rose and went into the Duhaisha.

March 8 Sunday, the 23rd [of Muḥarram]. The advance caravan of the pilgrimage arrived under its emir Tamurbughā aẓ-Ẓāhirī, the second executive secretary, as has been noted before; in company with him were Ṭūkh min Timrāz an-Nāṣirī [known as Buīnī Bāziq], an emir of the first class, and the Ḥanbalite Cadi Badr ad-Dīn al-Baghdādī.

*VIII, 62 March 9 * Monday, the 24th [of Muḥarram]. The emir of the litter caravan, the eunuch Fīrūz, chief eunuch and treasurer of the palace, arrived in Cairo with the remainder of the pilgrims.

March 11 Wednesday, the 26th [of Muḥarram]. The Sultan granted Ghars ad-Dīn Khalīl ibn Shāhīn ash-Shaikhī, one of the Damascus emirs of the first class, an emirate of the third class in addition to the emirate which he already had.

March 14 Saturday, the 29th [of Muḥarram]. Kāfūr al-Hindī aṭ-Ṭawāshī, head of the corps of wardrobe keepers and formerly an intimate cup bearer, died.

March 19 [Thursday, Ṣafar 4]. 'Abd al-'Azīz ibn Muḥammad aṣ-Ṣughaiyir put on the robe of superintendent of the Sultan's bureaus, in place of Jānibak al-Yashbakī, governor of Cairo, and became [at the same time] an emir of the horse, a chamberlain, and superintendent of bureaus, something the like of which we have not witnessed before—rather each one of them was independent by itself, and its rank as the early rulers placed it is well known.

March 21 Saturday, the 6th [of Ṣafar]. Dā'ud al-Maghribī, the merchant, died.

March 26 Thursday, the 11th [of Ṣafar]. Shams ad-Dīn Muḥammad ad-Daisaṭī al-Mālikī was imprisoned in Dailam Prison because of the charge against him brought by Cadi Nāṣir ad-Dīn Ibn al-Mukhalliṭa al-Mālikī in the council of Cadi [Shaikh of Islām Sa'd ad-Dīn] Ibn ad-Dairī al-Ḥanafī that he had said: "I do not accept bribes like Ibn al-Mukhalliṭa" and words like this; proof [of this charge] was established and he was imprisoned.

And on this day it was ordered that a royal edict be written naming Shams ad-Dīn Muḥammad ibn Sa'īd Ḥanbalite Cadi in Mecca in place of Sharīf Sirāj ad-Dīn because of the latter's death.

Also on this day the governor was ordered to beat the venerated slave Sa'dān, slave of Qāsim al-Mu'dhī the inspector-governor, and to display him in public, then place him in the Maqshara
VIII, 63 prison; and this was done. The story about this slave is a strange one, namely, that when his above mentioned master died in the first days of this year he left property, and wealth and children of his own loins. Zain ad-Dīn the major-domo wished to place a guard upon his possessions, as was customary in the case of others

like him, but this slave forbade him to do so and used harsh words in the manner of the Aḥmadīya dervishes, and went to extremes in doing so; he went to the sitting room of the major-domo and in talking to him various phrases were exchanged, including (some said) he cursed him, and others said that he threw off his turban from his head; the gist of it is that the major-domo threw the order at him, and the sergeant advanced toward him and intended to seize him, but was not able to move, as it was said, for I have not transferred this account from any one in whom I have confidence. Then when Zain ad-Dīn heard this he transmitted to his master what he had received, and this slave also went to the home of his master and stayed there, while the mention of him spread through Cairo; the men spoke about and elaborated the event, and the populace mentioned it aloud in the streets until everybody was talking about him, while people from every corner came to visit him and seek his blessing; men came to him, crowd after crowd, and this became so common that one could get to him only after much effort because of the size of the multitudes around him and the infatuation of the people for him. Then he began to seclude himself from them and only one of power or one who was of the foremost officials could reach him, and the quarter in which he was became like one of the places of amusement because of the multitudes of people, merchants, pleasure seekers, and visitors. This continued more than ten days, the condition growing and increasing, and a number of the greater emirs and government officials visited him while sufferers and those affected with chronic sicknesses sought him. Talk increased among them [about him] and what had happened to them in relation to him until his case reached the Sultan and he ordered the governor of Cairo and the grand chamberlain Tanbak to beat and imprison him. When the two entered to him Tanbak was too faint-hearted to strike him and did not dare take any action against him; this reached the Sultan, who banished him to the
VIII, 64 fortress of Damietta out of service, while the eunuch Khushqadam supervised the beating and imprisonment of the slave. Tanbak went to the fortress the next day, his escort being Jānibak al-Yashbakī the governor; and when the slave was imprisoned the governor on the next morning found at the gate of the prison crowds of those who had faith in the slave, and he beat some of them and imprisoned others.

March 28 Saturday, the 13th [of Ṣafar]. Shams ad-Dīn ad-Daisaṭī was released from Dailam Prison and there were brought against him before the Mālikite Cadi Walī ad-Dīn as-Sanbāṭī many charges the truth of which only God knows, but the opinion of the Cadi demanded his punishment; he punished him severely and shoved toward him a degree of shamelessness evidencing a complete purpose to ruin him in agreement with the feeling of Abu l-Khair an-Naḥḥās. Then he displayed him, naked on the streets with a herald proclaiming against him: "This is the punishment of one who flees from the law"; then he was imprisoned again. The reason for this and for the harshness of an-Naḥḥās against him was this: when Dā'ud al-Maghribī the merchant died and had named as executers of his estate among others Asanbughā aṭ-Ṭayyārī, chief head of guards, Jamāl ad-Dīn controller of privy funds; then this ad-Daisaṭī went and put a seal on the estate either because he was one of the executors or on behalf of one of them. This became known to an-Naḥḥās and a discussion on the subject arose between him and ad-Daisaṭī; ad-Daisaṭī swore that he had not sealed [the property]; Abu l-Khair went up and persuaded the Sultan that he should be the director of the estate, immediately went down and sent to ad-Daisaṭī one of the sergeants of the law; he [ad-Daisaṭī] fled [from the sergeant] and spurred his horse until he mounted the Citadel, entered to the Sultan, and asked that the complaint be before the Ḥanafite Cade; then went down, brought his charge against him before him [the Ḥanbalite Cadi]; and there occurred what we have narrated.

*VIII, 65 March 30 *Monday, the 15th [of Ṣafar]. Āqbirdī as-Sāqī, viceroy of the citadel of Aleppo, put on the robe of departure, and was ordered to go to Aleppo.

During these days Cadi Jalāl ad-Dīn Ibn Sa'ādāt ibn Ẓahīra was ordered to become Cadi of Mecca in place of Cadi Abu l-Yumn [Amīn ad-Dīn an-Nuwairī] after the latter's death; and Badr ad-Dīn Ḥasan ibn aṣ-Ṣawwāf was removed as Cadi of Ḥamā in favor of the very learned Shihāb ad-Dīn Aḥmad ibn 'Arabshāh ad-Dimashqī, [who was] requested in regard to [accepting] it.

March 30 Monday, the 15th [of Ṣafar] also. The Sultan demanded of the sons of the exiled Tanbak and his officials 30,000 dīnārs, that is, the remainder [of his debt]; then their affair resulted in the contribution of ten [thousand dīnārs more], it is said.

And on this date Ibn az-Zuwaigha, the Sultan's major-domo and the chamberlain in Ḥamā, was removed from office; Yaghmūr was appointed in his place and was granted all the positions of the deposed [Ibn az-Zuwaigha]. This Yaghmūr was one of the lowest class of the men; it was only a short time from the date when he had become a soldier and only a few years since he began to act as a servant in the service of the soldiers and intimate mamlūks, but he had by bribery and the intercession of Abu l-Khair an-Naḥḥās arrived [at his present position].

March 31 This day [the 16th of Ṣafar] ad-Daisaṭī was released from Dailam Prison.

April 2 [Ṣafar 18]. The eunuch 'Abd al-Laṭīf ar-Rūmī al-Īnālī died.

April 3 Friday, the 19th [of Ṣafar]. Jānibak al-Yashbakī the governor and market-inspector arrived from the fortress of Damietta after having taken Tanbak to it and received from him for having been his escort 1,000 dīnārs or less.

April 9 Thursday, the 25th [of Ṣāfar]. Zain ad-Dīn 'Umar Ibn al-Kharazī was appointed Shāfi'ite Cadi of Aleppo after the removal
VIII, 66 of Ibn Wajīh, and Bardbak al-'Ajamī al-Jakamī, an emir of the first class in Damascus, put on [the robe of] the emirate of the Damascus litter caravan and was ordered to proceed to Damascus.

April 14 I Rabī 1 was a Tuesday.

April 17 Friday, the 4th [of I Rabī'] corresponding to Barmūda 23, the Sultan put on his white clothing according to custom.

April 18 Saturday, the 5th [of I Rabī'). The removal of Ḥājj Īnāl al-Jakamī from the viceregency of al-Karak and the appointment of Ṭīghān, the Sultan's executive secretary in Damascus, in his place, were ordered. This continued until Abu l-Khair an-Naḥḥās, after the descent of the officials of the government, went up and spoke to the Sultan about the restoration of Īnāl; the Sultan gave a favorable reply to this and annuled what he had ordered—all this in less than half a day.

April 19 Sunday, the 6th [of I Rabī']. The Sultan celebrated the [Prophet's] birthday according to custom.

April 23 Thursday, the 10th [of I Rabī']. Burhān ad-Dīn as-Sūbīnī [the Shāfi'ite] was removed from the office of Cadi of Ṭarābulus and 'Izz ad-Dīn was restored to it for a sum of money which he paid.

April 24 Friday, the 11th [of I Rabī']. Shaikh Shams ad-Dīn ar-Rashīdī the preacher died.

April 29 Wednesday, the 16th [of I Rabī]. On this day was the beginning of the wedding of the Sultan's daughter to Uzbak. The Sultan on the day mentioned made a huge feast for the emirs in the Sultan's Park.

Thursday [I Rabī 17]. On the next day the Sultan prepared a great wedding celebration in the home of her uncle, Kamāl ad-Dīn al-Bārizī, the confidential secretary, in the Turner's Bazaar; this was the wedding ceremony for the women. The ceremony for the men was given in the home of the husband, Emir Uzbak, outside the Zuwaila Gates [that is] in his palace which had been built by Qīz Ṭūghān the major-domo. Uzbak at the end of the
VIII, 67 day mentioned, after the prayer of sunset, rode from his home and proceeded until he alighted in a court near the Tentmakers' Bazaar. Then after the last evening prayer of the day, with the emirs and notables walking before him, and the emirs carrying candles in front of his horse, he mounted wearing a double robe of embroidered satin. Kamāl ad-Dīn Ibn al-Bārizī, Muḥibb ad-

Dīn Ibn al-Ashqar, controller of the army, and Jamāl ad-Dīn, controller of privy funds, and others, walked before his horse until he reached the house of Kamāl ad-Dīn, dismounted, and entered the court of the wedding. The Sultan's daughter was displayed to him, and he went in to her. The wedding was not very magnificent, but was like the weddings of any prominent man; her trousseau, however, was most unusual; it was not carried on the heads of porters as was usually the case, but was taken out from the storehouses, then set up in "the house of the entrance" [of the husband to his bride]—I mean, the house of her uncle Kamāl ad-Dīn. When the arrangement of the trousseau was finished and the house was in order, the men at that time were given permission to enter and look at the trousseau; and the men saw garments, brocades, all kinds of furs, crystal vessels, ornaments of precious metal, and art objects of inscribed porcelain, which astounded and confounded them. I was among those who went in and I saw garments such as I had never seen before that date, despite the fact that I had seen not a little of this kind; for my sister, the Princess Fāṭima, was the wife of an-Nāṣir Faraj ibn Barqūq, and was the Grand Princess and mistress of the Court, until an-Nāṣir died while her husband. The first wife of my father was the Princess daughter of al-Manṣūr Ḥājjī, and the second was the Princess Ḥājj Mulk, daughter of Ibn Qarā and wife of aẓ-Ẓāhir Barqūq. I saw their garments and goods and precious objects from one time to the next until today, and they were very many; but with all this I have not seen—nay more, I have not heard of, a trousseau like this one, not in quantity and
VIII, 68 not in beauty, nor in what it contained of all kinds of brocaded drapes, scarves decorated with hugh pearls, and varieties of art objects which no princess before her had attained.

April 30 Thursday [I Rabīʻ 17]. Khushqadam [an-Nāṣirī al-Mu'ayyadī] arrived in Cairo and kissed the ground; he was granted an emirate of the first class in place of Tanbak, as has been noted before. And Tanbak an-Naurūzī al-Khaṣṣakī was invested with the viceregency of Ṣahyūn after the removal of Bardbak al-ʻAjamī as-Saifī Ṭarabāi, an emir of Ṭarābulus.

May 7 Thursday, the 24th [of I Rabīʻ]. Muḥibb ad-Dīn Ibn Shiḥna, Ḥanafite Cadi in Aleppo, arrived at the exalted gates, and stood before the Sultan.

May 12 Tuesday, the 29th [of I Rabīʻ]. ʻAlī Bāi as-Sāqī al-Ashrafī died.

May 14 II Rabīʻ 1 was a Wednesday [Thursday]. On this day a proclamation was made in Cairo that the new coppers should be at 36 dirhams a pound after they had been at 42 [dirhams].

And on this day the Sultan designated 110 intimate mamlūks to guard the sea coasts against the European marauders.

May 15 [II Rabī' 2 (1)]. The Sultan designated a number of other Sultan's mamlūks, added to those designated the previous day, to guard the frontiers.

May 16 Saturday, the 4th [3rd of II Rabī']. A proclamation was made that the new coppers should be at their first price again.

May 18 Monday, the 6th [5th of II Rabī']. Jamāl ad-Dīn [Yūsuf ibn Kātib Jakam], controller of privy funds, put on the robe of favor after he had been obliged to pay [to the royal treasury] 100,000 dīnārs through the intervention of Abu l-Khair an-Naḥḥās, for he continued to inflame the mind of the Sultan against him, arouse his cupidity for his wealth and recommend to him his seizure and mulcting until the Sultan yielded to him and accepted his words, and from that time the status of Jamāl ad-Dīn began to decline while Abu l-Khair's increased until the latter became the real
VIII, 69 ruler in the realm, and his position grew considerably in power and importance through this event because he advanced beyond all the other bureau officials and ruined them all except this Jamāl ad-Dīn; for the authoritative word in the government remained between the two and they became like two race horses, each racing against the other in whatever they aimed at, until at this time authority was confined to an-Naḥḥās.

May 18 On the date mentioned Zain ad-Dīn 'Abd al-Qādir ibn ar-Rassām al-Ḥamawī was appointed controller of the army of Aleppo in place of Ibn ash-Shiḥna because of the latter's removal.

May 19 Tuesday, the 7th [6th of II Rabī']. The Sultan ordered that Ibn ash-Shiḥna be placed under guard and that he be taken to the house of Daulāt Bāi the executive secretary because of the charge brought by one of the Aleppans against him.

May 20 Wednesday, the 8th [7th of II Rabī']. The wedding took place of Tanam, emir of the council, to the Sultan's sister, who had come [to Cairo] in the preceding year from the land of Circassia.

May 21 Thursday, the 9th [8th of II Rabī']. Kamāl ad-Ḍīn Ibn al-Bārizī was removed as confidential secretary because 'Abd al-'Azīz ibn Muḥammad aṣ-Ṣughaiyir, when he had gone to the fortress of Damietta in Rabī' I taking with him on behalf of the Sultan, as was the custom in the case of emirs out of service, a horse for the chamberlain Tanbak, there was written at his band an order the contents of which was to take the rent of the monopolized lands in the fortress [of Damietta]. And when he went there he was rough and harsh and tyrannical toward the people of Damietta, forcing them to act beyond their ability and wearying them; then one of the populace of Damietta revolted against him, stoned him and wounded him in the forehead or the nostril, with a rock. A report of this reached the Sultan, and what the one mentioned ['Abd al-'Azīz] had done displeased him; and he ordered that he be

brought [to Cairo]. Sha'bān al-Barīdī went for this purpose after the Sultan had given him twenty Zāhirī [dīnārs] from the royal
May 21 treasury. Sha'bān left that same day for [Damietta] Fortress to bring to Cairo the individual mentioned.

VIII, 70 The Sultan then turned his attention to Kamāl ad-Dīn the confidential secretary, upraided and, after reproving him for the order which he had given, spoke roughly to him and said to him: "I did not order any of this." He [Cadi Kamāl ad-Dīn] began to dispute with him and was so earnest that the truth of what he said became apparent; this irritated the Sultan and he removed him from office; the Cadi went to his home out of service, but the chief government officials flocked to him; there was much talk about him, and he remained thus until what was to come.

May 23 Saturday, the 11th [10th of II Rabī']. The Sultan ordered the removal of Muḥammad ibn Tūqān ibn Nu'air from the emirate of the Āl Faḍl Arabs and he established in his place Ghannām, the son of his uncle; Khushkaldī the executive secretary took the diploma to him.

May 25 Monday, the 13th [12th of II Rabī']. Prince Muḥammad, the Sultan's son, died at less than ten months of age; and Sūdūn al-Īnālī Qarāqāsh, an emir of the third class and head of guards, was ordered banished to Jerusalem because the Sultan had received a report that the Muḥārib Arabs, who were hostile to the government, had come to the district of Buḥaira, and to fight them he sent Jarbāsh Kurd and the mentioned Sūdūn; the two left Cairo that same day, Saturday the 11th, and with those with them attacked the Muḥārib Arabs in a raid, conquered and took possession of the property of the Muḥārib, drove the Muḥārib themselves away; they took the property and returned toward the Jīza shore until they reached Minbāba, opposite Būlāq. Jarbāsh and Sūdūn crossed the Nile, but left the property of the Muḥārib on the shore of Minbāba, for the party was convinced that the Muḥārib had fled from them and furthermore they had come under the Sultan's protection. But in the space of only a moment there were the Muḥārib, who had wheeled their horses into a gallop, taken possession of their property and recovered it together with the baggage of the two emirs, and had reached the Nile—nay more, the boats which were used for crossing, and had taken of what was there whatever they had the strength to take; this was an event
VIII, 71 the like of which we had not seen or heard of, namely, that the Muḥārib Arabs had reached Minbāba and done anything like this. And when the Sultan learned of this it angered him and he ordered the banishment of Sūdūn; and as for Jarbāsh, he bestowed him on his wife, the Princess Shaqrā, daughter of an-Nāṣir Faraj ibn Barqūq.

On this day also Ibn al-Hamām al-Maqdisī was appointed Sultan's major-domo in Damascus after the removal of Asandamur al-Arghūn Shāwī. And Cadi Zain ad-Dīn Faraj ibn as-Sābiq was appointed confidential secretary of Ḥamā as he had been before. Also Badr ad-Dīn Ḥasan ibn 'Alī ibn Muḥammad ibn aṣ-Ṣawwāf, the Ḥanafite Cadi of Ḥamā, arrived [in Cairo].

May 28 Thursday, the 16th [15th of II Rabī']. Kamāl ad-Dīn al-Bārizī put on the robe of continuance in office. And 'Alā' ad-Dīn 'Alī ibn 'Abd Allāh the warden of the armory, known as Ibn Khawājā, died. Also a number of the people of Damietta came to Cairo on account of a complaint against 'Abd al-'Azīz ibn Muḥammad aṣ-Ṣughaiyir; they were ordered to ascend to the Citadel on Saturday to argue the truth of the complaint.

June 5 Friday, the 24th [23rd of II Rabī']. The wife of Qānibai the Circassian died. And 'Abd al-'Azīz aṣ-Ṣughaiyir ascended to the Citadel and stood at the gate of the Duhaisha; he was not given permission to enter, but was prevented from doing so. The matter weighed upon him, and anxiety entered his mind because he had falsely written in his own handwriting an order in the name of the Sultan, and also because of what he had done with the people of the fortress. So he went down immediately and threw himself upon an-Naḥḥās, who advised him to go up on Saturday and dispute with his adversaries before the Sultan, which he did. When he stood before the Sultan, the latter ordered him to be under guard until, after being revised and threatened with beating and imprisonment, he should return to the people of Damietta what he had taken from them.

June 6 Saturday [II Rabī' 24]. A council was convened with the four Cadis before the Sultan on the matter of Badr ad-Dīn Ibn aṣ-Ṣawwāf, Cadi of Ḥamā; it was charged against him that in Ḥamā there was a small mosque which had been ruined in the war with Tamerlane in 803, and that he [Ibn aṣ-Ṣawwāf] had transported it and built out of its ruins a mosque in Ḥamā. The council was

VIII, 72 ended without any proof, and [Ibn aṣ-Ṣawwāf] went down under guard, until finally there was paid to the treasury 3,500 dīnārs, which was the sum sought. I say, he had a habit of doing this hateful deed ever since he was appointed Cadi of Ḥamā, paying for an office whatever sum occurred to him, and I do not know from where he would acquire such a large sum when he paid it—but God knows best.

June 1 Monday, the 20th [19th of II Rabī']. Ḥusām ad-Dīn ibn Buraiṭi' was appointed Ḥanafite Cadi in Damascus after the removal of Ḥamīd ad-Dīn [an-Nu'mānī].

June 1 Monday, the 20th [19th] of II Rabī'. 'Alī Bāi's emirate of the first class was bestowed upon Īnāl as-Sāqī aẓ-Ẓāhirī, who had previously been banished to Ṭarābulus and was known as Īnāl

Khawand because in his youth he was handsome. And 'Alā' ad-Dīn 'Alī al-Bunduqdārī was appointed third warden of the armory in place of 'Alī ibn Khawājā, who had previously died.

And the command went out to 'Abd al-'Azīz ibn Muḥammad aṣ-Ṣughaiyir to remain at his home and not ride a horse; also that he should return quietly what he had taken from Mu'īn ad-Dīn al-Abraṣ ad-Dīmyāṭī and what he had taken from the Dimyāṭians, otherwise he would be beaten with cudgels; he immediately obeyed.

And Mubārak Shāh, viceroy of Jerusalem, came to the royal gates, and was on the same day removed in favor of Saif ad-Dīn Iyās al-Bajāsī al-Khāṣṣakī, both of whom were without distinction in the government.

June 2 Tuesday, the 21st [20th of II Rabī']. Orders went out again to 'Abd al-'Azīz ibn aṣ-Ṣughaiyir to give back the goods, etc. which he had taken from the sons of Tanbak al-Bardbakī the chamberlain; he returned this completely and entirely.

June 8 Monday, the 27th [26th of II Rabī']. Muḥibb ad-Dīn [Muḥammad] ibn Maulānā Zādah al-Aqṣarā'ī was dismissed from the position of Sultan's prayer leader. And orders went out for the return
*VIII, 73 of Ibn ash-Shiḥna *to Aleppo under the guard of Īnāl Bāi al-Khaṣṣakī; then this was annuled on condition that he should remain as he had been before and pay 50,000 dīnārs.

And on it the Cadi of Sawākin came to Cairo and mentioned to His Royal Highness that the Abyssinians had built about two hundred ships for raiding the Mohammedans, and that that their purpose was to cut off the flow of the Nile and divert it from them.

June 9 Tuesday, the 28th [27th of II Rabī']. An extremely disgraceful event occurred in Cairo: Shaikh 'Alī the market inspector attacked the home of the very learned shaikh Qawām ad-Dīn Ḥusain al-'Ajamī al-Ḥanafī after arranging a stratagem against him. This was that previously he sent to him a Persian individual under the pretence that he was one of the students; and when this man had secured a firm position with the shaikh and used to go up to him without asking his permission, he carried to him on this day instruments for making false coins, such as a die and a finger and others, in a leather bag, and said to the shaikh: "See, sir, what I do." The shaikh stood up, preparing to ride to one of his instruments, while the student prevented him from going and prolonged talking with him until the market inspector (who was mentioned above [Shaikh 'Alī]) surprised the two as they were thus, seized the bag referred to and also Qawām ad-Dīn, but let the student go, until he fled and left his bag behind; he [the market inspector] took Qawām ad-Dīn and the bag up to the Sultan after writing a letter with the implication that he had found the instruments for falsification in his possession. The Sultan ordered his imprisonment in the Tower of the Citadel.

The cause of the emnity of the market inspector for Qawām ad-Dīn was the fact that the Sultan, when he had earlier banished him, had bestowed on Qawām ad-Dīn the market inspector's cloister looking under the Rumaila near the Maṣna'. Then intercession was made for the market inspector and he returned to his office of shaikh and other positions, but he hated Qawām ad-Dīn
*VIII, 74 for this reason and desired to *dishonor him in the Sultan's estimation, and so arranged this plot.

June 10 Wednesday, the 29th [28th of II Rabī']. The market inspector was invested with maintenance in the office of supreme shaikh of the Siryāqaus Monastery in place of Shihāb ad-Dīn Aḥmad ibn Muḥibb ad-Dīn ibn al-Ashqar because of the latter's removal.

And in this month the report came from the viceroy of Ayās that in the city of Ayās a violent earthquake had occurred from which a number of buildings had fallen, and from the violence of the quake a large wall of its citadel also had fallen.

June 12 I Jumādā 1 was a Thursday [Friday]. Sawinjbughā al-Yūnusī, an emir of the third class and head of guards, was appointed on this day emir of the Rajabī pilgrims.

June 13 Saturday, the 3rd [2nd of I Jumādā]. The Sultan ordered that Badr ad-Dīn Maḥmūd ibn 'Ubaid Allāh al-Ardbīlī al-Ḥanafī, one of the Ḥanafite deputy cadis, and Shihāb ad-Dīn Aḥmad ibn al-'Arīf, with a number of others, be imprisoned in the Maqshara because they had borne witness before the Badr ad-Dīn just mentioned to the pious endowment of [the house of] Asanbāi as-Sāqī aẓ-Ẓāhirī Jaqmaq, and the Cadi had decreed it without either he or the witnesses knowing that the Sultan had wished the solution of the truth and the seizure of the house belonging to Asanbāi by whatever way it might be; so whatever God wishes comes to pass.

June 15 Monday, the 5th [4th of I Jumādā]. The Sultan took Qawām ad-Dīn (mentioned a little above) from the Tower; in full view of the public he cudgelled him on the shoulders and ordered him to go down to Maqshara Prison while the proclamation was made concerning him: "This is the reward of one who makes counterfeits or other things of this class." This was after the Sultan on the day before had convened a council of the four Cadis and summoned the [defendant] mentioned; nothing had been confirmed against him nor did he confess anything which justified punishment; all he said was: "This is a trick which the market inspector devised against me; but the Sultan examines into the truth of my statement, then he does with me whatever he desires." But he [the Sultan] paid no attention to his remarks and on the morrow did what we have related; and what happened to him displeased the men extremely.

*VIII, 75 *And on this day Badr ad-Dīn ibn 'Ubaid Allāh was freed from the Maqshara and went to the home of the adjutant of the army.

And Jamāl ad-Dīn al-Bā'ūnī was removed as Cadi of Damascus

in favor of Burhān ad-Dīn as-Sūbīnī, who had previously been removed [as Cadi] from Ṭarābulus.

June 16 Tuesday, the 6th [5th of II Jumādā]. The Sultan summoned before him Badr ad-Dīn ibn 'Ubaid Allāh and the witnesses mentioned above; and spoke to them about their evidence in regard to the pious foundation; they confirmed what they had said, and said also that there was a letter concerning the pious foundation of the house, which letter was in the possession of Ibn al-Aujāqī, who was traveling in the Ḥijāz. When the Sultan heard what they said he ordered their return to the Maqshara. The Ḥanafite Cadi Sa'd ad-Dīn Ibn ad-Dairī spoke about them, but the Sultan rebuked him and paid no attention to what he said; so they were taken to the Maqshara and imprisoned there again. A letter was written to Mecca to send Shihāb ad-Dīn Aḥmad ibn al-Aujāqī from there to Cairo in company with Jānibak, superintendant of Bundar Judda.

And on this day a decree was written for the appointment of Muḥammad ibn Tūqān ibn Nu'air to the emirate of the Āl Faḍl, and his uncle's son, Ghannām, was removed from the position—all this happened before the arrival to Ghannām of the report of the appointment, so the appointment and removal occurred while he did not know of it.

June 18 Thursday, the 8th [7th of I Jumādā]. Muḥibb ad-Dīn Ibn ash-Shiḥnā put on the robe of the office of Ḥanafite Cadi of Aleppo and [it was ordered that] the office of confidential secretary there should belong to his son; and as-Sūbīnī was invested with the appointment as Cadi of Damascus in place of al-Bā'ūnī, as has been noted before.

June 19 Friday, the 9th [8th of I Jumādā]. A proclamation was issued concerning the coppers which had been coined of old that they should be at 36 [dirhams] per pound, while the newly coined

*VIII, 76 [coppers] should be by tale; and that the silver *coined with the Sultan's die at 24 dirhams should remain as they were, while the silver coins outside his coinage should be at 20 [dirhams].

June 20 Saturday, the 10th [9th of I Jumādā], corresponding to Ba'ūna 27, one of the Coptic months. The measure of the Nile was taken, and the minimum came out as 6 cubits, 15 fingers.

June 21–25 [I Jumādā 11–15]. Among the unusual events of these days was that the imported mamlūks prevented most of the bureau officials from riding horses, so that scholars and notable administrators of the government rode asses. The mamlūks stood in the paths and streets, and attacked any official whom they caught riding on a horse; and the followers of Abu l-Khair an-Naḥḥās disappeared entirely from view.

June 27 Saturday, the 17th [16th of I Jumādā]. A report reached Cairo of the rebellion and revolt of Baighūt al-A'raj, viceroy of Ḥamā, and his adherence to al-'Ijl ibn Nu'air.

June 28 Sunday, the 18th [17th of I Jumādā]. The Sultan went down from the Citadel with all his emirs and notables of government, without their formal attire, and he preceded to Būlāq to view the bridge which he had ordered built between aṭ-Ṭunbadīya and Ma'ṣarat al-Khalīfa. He viewed it while riding on his horse; he admired it and invested with robes the architect 'Alī ibn Iskandar, foster son of Ibn al-Faisī, and Ibn Ẓahīr, and others of those who had supervised its building; he then returned and passed through Cairo until he ascended the Citadel.

July 2 [Thursday, I Jumādā 22 (21)]. Shaikh 'Alī [aṭ-Ṭawīl al-Khurāsānī] al-'Ajamī was restored to the office of market-inspector after the removal of Jānibak al-Wālī; and the Sultan released Ibn 'Ubaid Allāh from the Maqshara Prison.

*VIII, 77 July 3 *Friday, the 23rd [22nd of I Jumādā]. Cairo was disturbed by the report of the rebellion of Julbān the next day; but the next morning, Saturday, the falsity of this report became clear.

July 6 Monday, the 26th [25th of I Jumādā]. An order was issued for the removal of 'Abd Allāh, the inspector-governor of Sharqīya and his presence [in Cairo] in irons, because of the charge against him brought by Abu l-Khair an-Naḥḥās; and his emirate and office were granted to Asandamur al-Jaqmaqī, one of the emirs of the third class and head of guards, added to what he then held; and from this anyone who desired harm for an-Naḥḥās learned a lesson.

July 6 [I Jumādā 26 (25)]. Qānibāi al-Ḥasanī al-Mu'ayyadī, an emir of the third class in Egypt, was ordered to become commander in chief of Ḥamā in place of Sunqur as-Saifī Jār Quṭlū.

July 7 Tuesday, the 27th [26th of I Jumādā]. 'Abd Allāh, the inspector-governor, came to Cairo and settled in the home of Zain ad-Dīn the major-domo; favor came to him the next day on payment of a sum of money which he paid.

July 9 Thursday, the 29th [28th of I Jumādā]. The Sultan granted the emirate of Qānibāi al-Ḥasanī to his mamlūk Shāhīn aẓ-Ẓāhirī the cupbearer despite the fact that he was a disgrace to mankind; Saif ad-Dīn Barqūq aẓ-Ẓāhirī was appointed a cupbearer in his place. And the eunuch Surūr aṭ-Ṭarabā'ī was appointed shaikh of the servitor negroes in the Prophet's holy city in place of the eunuch Fāris ar-Rūmī al-Ashrafī because of his removal; then this was annuled on Saturday.

July 10 [I Jumādā 29]. When an-Naḥḥās went up to the Citadel on this day also his position improved greatly and he became important in the eyes of the men, particularly since the Sultan on this day had ordered the appointment of [Abu l-Fatḥ] aṭ-Ṭayyībī to his office and had given consent to him [to an-Naḥḥās] to take a number of objects by which the favor of the Sultan for him became apparent; the men then flocked to his doors, crowd after crowd,

especially when the Sultan came to hate al-Balāṭunusī after first having favored him, and similarly when he removed 'Abd Allāh
VIII, 78 the inspector-governor for his sake. He continued thus from the day of his ascent [to the Citadel], which was Thursday, until the coming Thursday, the 29th, when this misfortune occurred to him, and Sharaf ad-Dīn al-Anṣarī went on his mission, as we have related.

In this month the price of crops was as follows: Wheat, 500 [dirhams] and down, after it had reached 850; beans, 360 and less; barley, 230 to 250; fine flour, 170 per baṭṭa.

The month passed with no one of the officials able to ride a horse—they took to riding mules and asses, excepting the confidential secretary, his deputy, the controller of the army, of privy funds, and of the stables, the vizier, the major-domo, the scribe of the bureau of mamlūks and of fodder, so that one of the deputies of the law said to me: "These purchased mamlūks have joined us to the protected people, in our failure to ride horses—there is no power save in God."

II Jumādā 1 was a Saturday [Sunday].

July 12 On this day the Inspector 'Abd Allāh put on the robe of continuance in office, after paying a considerable sum of money.

July 12 Sunday, the 2nd [the 1st of II Jumādā]. The gift of Julbān, viceroy of Damascus, went up [to the Sultan] with its executive secretary and emir of the horse; it was a huge gift containing more than 200 horses, which included two with gold housing, and almost 300 porters of wool, various species of fur, Ba'labakkī stuff, satin,
VIII, 79 strips of silk, and about 10,000 dīnārs in gold. And during these days the messenger of the viceroy of Damascus put on the robe of departure; from the day of his arrival until this day he had not been invested with any robe.

When the Sultan took possession of the horses of the above mentioned Abu l-Khair he distributed them to whomever he chose.

"With this ended the days among whose people the misfortunes of some were advantage to others."

And on this day also a report came from the viceroy of Aleppo, Qānibāi al-Ḥamzāwī, at the hand of his head of guards, that Jahañ Shāh ibn Quarā Yūsuf intended to march against Jahān Kīr ibn 'Ali Bak ibn Qarā Yuluk, and that Jahān Kīr had no escape except to come to Aleppan territory, where there was no army to turn him away. The arrival of the messenger occurred after ten days; an answer was written for him, also a number of orders for the departure of the viceroys of Syria to the borders of Aleppan lands.

July 14 Tuesday, the 4th [3rd of II Jumādā]. Kamāl ad-Dīn Ibn al-Bārizī, the confidential secretary, was ordered banished to Damascus; he immediately went down from the Citadel and, without

entering his home, set out for Damascus. But when he arrived outside Cairo he was ordered to return; so he went back home against his will, for his only desire was to get away from Egypt and rest himself from what he was suffering. The cause of this was that when the Sultan, as was his custom, sat on the dais in the Park and documents concerning the army were read to him, he became angry at Ibn al-Ashqar, abused him roundly, and attempted more than once to strike him with his poniard. Then a report reached the Sultan that Qāsim ibn Qarā Yuluk had almost reached Siryāqaus Monastery; the Sultan was astonished at his arrival there, because when he left Diyār Bakr after having been with his brother Jahān
VIII, 80 Kīr and, disagreeing with him, had gone to Abulustān, to Sulaimān ibn Nāṣir ad-Dīn Bak ibn Dulghādir; Sulaimān had sent to ask permission of the Sultan for Qāsim to come to Egypt; the Sultan did not give permission for this, but ordered him (Qāsim) to continue his stay with him (Jahān Kīr), writing to him to this effect; he remained with him only a few days, when news reached him [the Sultan] of his arrival. He (the Sultan) was angered, and asked the confidential secretary: "Did you write him about his coming?" The secretary answered: "Yes," although this was not a fact; he merely wished to protect himself, fearing that there might be some hidden blame attached to him in this. The Sultan then asked for the original draft of the letter, but did not find in it the permission for him to come. Thereupon he ordered the secretary to be beaten; and Barsbāi al-Īnālī al Mu'ayyadī, the second emir of the horse, struck him once, and he was expelled in flight from the Sultan's presence.

And on this day Zain ad-Dīn Ibn al-Kuwaiz was ordered handed over to the governor to have extracted from him the remainder of what he was obligated to pay to the Sultan.

July 16 [II Jumādā 6 (5)]. Qāsim ibn Qarā Yuluk came to Cairo in company with the ambassador of Sulaimān ibn Dulghādir, stood before the Sultan, kissed the ground, then went down to the Race Course.

July 19 Sunday, the 9th [8th of II Jumādā]. The master architect Muḥammad aṣ-Ṣughaiyir, one of the chamberlains, and his son 'Abd al-'Azīz, who before this date had been sent away, were ordered banished to Qūṣ; then intercession was made for both of them, with the proviso that they should be obligated to pay some money—and how excellent this would have been if it had continued!

July 20 Monday, the 10th [9th of II Jumādā]. Muḥibb ad-Dīn Ibn al-Ashqar put on the robe of continuance in office and to Fīrūz an-Naurūzī the treasurer were returned the pious foundations of the holy places which an-Naḥḥās had taken possession of in the past year. And Asandamur al-Arghūn Shāwī was invested with the appointment as Sultan's major-domo and superintendent of the Jordan Valley in Damascus in place of ['Abd al-Wāḥid] Humām ad-Dīn on the payment of about 10,000 dīnārs; and the arrest of Ibn al-Humām was ordered.

*VIII, 81 *Tuesday, the 11th [10th of II Jumādā]. Muḥibb ad-Dīn ibn ash-Shiḥna put on [a robe] on his return to the office of controller of the army of Aleppo in place of 'Abd al-Qādir ibn ar-Rassām, added to the offices of Cadi and confidential secretary there, which he already held; [this was] after Ibn ash-Shīḥna had agreed to pay a large sum of money, and in addition, to provide the barley for the Sultan's mamlūks if they went on a campaign to Aleppo territory.

This report [that Abu l-Khair an Naḥḥās was insane], though it was not true, was plausible, for he had at first been lowly then exalted until he ruled Egypt—and more, all of Damascus and Aleppo territory, and became the final authority in all the realm, knowing a degree of power and effective authority such as none beside him has known in our time; [I say this] despite my knowledge of those who preceded him. Then God returned him to a condition lower even than that in which he had been at first; for he was now poor with only meager resources, and became as you see, deprived of the wealth and properties which had been his, while his possessions were in the hands of the merchants and he himself was in prison and in chains, ready for death—we ask God for a happy future in this world and the next; it has been said: Who tastes riches after poverty dies with the fear of wants in his heart."

July 22 Wednesday, the 12th [11th of II Jumādā]. The Sultan reviewed his intimate mamlūks and designated 350 of them to journey in the expedition. Then he ordered the review of the Sultan's mamlūks on the coming Sunday, to designate a number of them also; and he ordered that the commander of this army should be the commander-in-chief Īnāl, and he ordered to accompany him Daulāt Bāi, the grand executive's secretary, one of the emirs of the first class; and of the emirs of the second class al-Yūnusī an-Nāṣirī and Barsbāi al-Īnālī al Mu'ayyadī; and of the emirs of the third class;
VIII, 82 Uzbak min Ṭaṭakh aẓ-Ẓāhirī, Asanbāi al-Jamālī as-Sāqī aẓ-Ẓāhirī —and Bardbak al-Bajmaqdār. These three were his own mamlūks; also Yashbak al-Faqīh and Yalbāi al-Inālī al-Mu'ayyadi.

July 23 Then the next day, Thursday the 13th [12th of II Jumādā] commander-in-chief Īnāl spoke with the Sultan about the small number of emirs and others of the army going with him; and what he said was this: "O our Lord Sultan, the enemy is a foreign rebel and his army is large, while this army, because of its smallness, is not able to repulse him." This displeased the Sultan, his anger became intense, and he said to him; "You have no interest in the expedition," and other remarks like this. The commander-in-chief withheld reply to this and said simply: "The order is the order of the Sultan, and his command is to be obeyed; his opinion is better than what we opine." The interview ended, and the Sultan entered the Park; but he approved the remark of the commander-in-chief and designated also of emirs of the first class Asanbughā aṭ-Ṭayyārī and ordered Bardbak al-Bajmaqdār not to go on the expedition, because of his lack of importance, and did not designate any one in his place.

And on this day also Bardbak at-Tājī al-Khāṣṣakī put on the robe of departure by sea to Mecca, to become controller of the sacred territory, its market inspector and its superintendent of constructions, in place of Saif ad-Dīn Bairam Khujā al-Ashrafī al-Faqīh; with him went a number of builders and others.

And on this day [at Cairo] Abu l-Fatḥ aṭ-Ṭayyibī arrived from Damascus in a wretched condition.

July 25 Saturday evening, the 15th [14th of II Jumādā], there was an eclipse of the moon. The eclipse had begun at twilight, [and continued] until most of the body of the moon was eclipsed and what was left of it increased in redness so that it had no more light and the stars shone in the sky just as during the last nights of the month; this continued until about an hour after nightfall; then it began little by little to become bright again.

*VIII, 83 *On Saturday also, agreeing with [Coptic] Misrā, an increase in the Nile of five fingers was announced, to complete five cubits and 25 fingers.

On this day also the Sultan released the very learned Shaikh Qawām ad-Dīn al-'Ajamī from al-Maqshara Prison.

July 26 Sunday, the 16th [15th II Jumādā]. The Sultan sat in the Park and reviewed the Sultans' mamlūks; he designated more than 120 of them, added to more previously designated, and designated also of the emirs Marijān al-'Ādilī, deputy commander of the mamlūks, and another.

July 28 Tuesday, the 18th [17th II Jumādā]. Ṣārim ad-Dīn Ibrāhīm ibn Baighūt, viceroy of Ḥamā who had revolted that day, was given a moderate beating before the Sultan, and in the presence of his father's messengers; then he was returned to his prison in the Tower of the Citadel. The occasion of this movement was that his father had on the day before sent to the Sultan a dromedary messenger asking from his amnesty and the release of this son of his. The dromedary rider also brought a letter from Julbān, viceroy of Damascus, containing a plea in behalf of Baighūt, to which the Sultan paid no attention, but gave this boy the cudgeling we have described without any fault on his part—there is no power except in God!

Aug. 1 Saturday, the 22nd [21st II Jumādā]. The Confidential Secretary, Ibn al-Bārizī. put on the robe of continuance in his office after having remained at home away from it a long time, as we have narrated; while his deputy, Ma'īn ad-Dīn 'Abd al-Laṭīf Ibn al-'Ajamī, administered the office during these days.

Also Niẓām ad-Dīn 'Umar ibn Mufliḥ was invested with the return to the Ḥanbalite judiciary in Damascus.

Also Bardbak at-Tājī and the builders and others with him, set out by sea for Mecca.

Aug. 3 Monday, the 24th [23rd of II Jumādā]. Īnāl Bāi al-Khāṣṣakī set
VIII, 84 out for Damascus; he was accompanied by Abu l-Fatḥ aṭ-Ṭayyibī in a wretched condition, to examine into the facts of his case and do to him what the law required.

Then the next day [II Jumādā 25], he [Chief Cadi Sharaf ad-Dīn al-Munāwī] sent to him [to 'Izz ad-Dīn Ibn al-Bisāṭī] to cause him to cease officiating in his judicial court; he rose immediately, made the rounds of the officials, informed them of what had happened to him, and requested that a session with the four Cadis and the prominent lawyers be convened in the Park in the presence of the
Aug. 5 Sultan on Wednesday, the 26th [25th of II Jumādā]. When the court had been convened and the Cadis were present with the witnesses who had testified against an-Naḥḥās, likewise the complainant Sharīf [Ahmad] Ibn al-Miṣbaḥ the Sultan asked the Shāfi'ite Cadi: "Has the charge of the infidelity of an-Naḥḥas been confirmed?" He replied: "The Mālikite Cadi has the charge." The Mālikite Cadi gave a long discourse the gist of which was that nothing had been fixed against him in his [the Mālikite's] presence. When the Sultan heard what he said he summoned 'Izz ad-Dīn al-Bisāṭī, who arose and stood before him in order to speak, but the Shāfi'ite Cadi anticipated him and said: "His wrong doing has been fixed before men." The Sultan turned toward 'Izz ad-Dīn and said: "I have known you for forty years—take you him to the Maqshara." Then he summoned him again and he repeated what he had said; then he ordered him to be imprisoned after reproving him. Then he summoned the rest of the witnesses namely Ibn al-Kaum Rīshī and others and, before he heard what they said, he ordered all of them likewise to be imprisoned as the Maqshara. When Sharīf, the complainant, heard what had happened he spoke, and said: "Our lord Sultan, the witnesses who testified to the charge concerning 'Izz ad-Dīn repudiated their testimony." The Sultan paid no regard to what he said but said to him: "You said to me yesterday that the Mālikite Cadi took a bribe in the case

of an-Naḥḥās and cancelled this order—so take him also to the Maqshara!" So they took all of them down and they were imprisoned there with the criminals.

*VIII, 85 *So notice the action of this world toward debtors; excellent is the verse of him who recited the verses [wāfir meter; rhyming words: wafatkī, mubkī] I see the world say to its lovers: "beware, beware of my reproach and my rashness; let not a smile from me deceive you, for my speech may cause laughing while my deed brings weeping."